THE CHRISTIAN VISION

MORALITY AND THE MARKETPLACE

THE CHRISTIAN VISION

MORALITY AND THE MARKETPLACE

Michael Bauman, Executive Editor
Lissa Roche and William Koshelnyk, General Editors

Hillsdale College Press
Hillsdale, Michigan 49242

Hillsdale College Press

Books by the Hillsdale College Press include *The Christian Vision* series; the *Champions of Freedom* series; and other works.

The Christian Vision Series
MORALITY AND THE MARKETPLACE
© 1994 by the Hillsdale College Press
Hillsdale, Michigan 49242

Printed in the United States of America

Photo: Appalight Photography, Spencer, WV

First printing 1994

Library of Congress Catalog Card Number 94-077458
ISBN 0-916308-70-7

Contents

READINGS

Introduction

When we judge different economic systems, we tend to focus on their practical differences. Which system provides greater prosperity? Who benefits most? Rarely do we ask: Which system is more moral? Which is truer to human nature? But such questions are, or ought to be, fundamental to economics. While every system has its theories, principles, models, graphs, and formulas, it also has its underlying values. Not surprisingly, one of the first and greatest economists was also a moral philosopher. Adam Smith argued in *Wealth of Nations* (1776) that spontaneous decisions, unrestricted competition, the division of labor, and freedom of transaction are tangible expressions of free will. He pointed out that capitalism emulates the Judeo-Christian tradition by rewarding responsibility, accountability, thrift, industry, and charity, further noting that self-interest and the profit motive actually can and do benefit society as if an "invisible hand" were at work directing it.

Today, free market advocates like Amway cofounder Rich DeVos (father of one of the contributors to this volume) call this "compassionate capitalism." Ronald Nash added in an earlier volume in this Christian Vision series: "Capitalism ... recognizes several necessary conditions for the kind of voluntary relationships it recommends. One of these presuppositions is the existence of inherent human rights, such as the right to make decisions, the right to be free, the right to hold property, and the right to exchange.... Capitalism is quite simply the most moral system, and the most equitable system of economic exchange."

1

But the dominant view among many modern economists, journalists, and politicians is that capitalism only rewards greed and creates economic injustice. They contend that a government-managed economy—they shun the term "socialism"—must be adopted in order to eliminate the "unfair" advantages of one economic class over another and redistribute wealth. Central planning and regulation, they say, are also necessary to prevent people from acting in their own narrow self-interest and to end the "chaos" of the market.

On every issue society faces, from the environment to homelessness, from inflation to taxes, the dividing line is between those who regard individual freedom as the best policy and those who advocate more government. In each case, it comes down to a matter of profoundly different values and views about the morality of the marketplace.

The essays in this seventh volume of the Christian Vision series were originally presented during Hillsdale College's Center for Constructive Alternatives seminar "Morality and the Marketplace" on September 19-23, 1993.

July, 1994   The Editors
Hillsdale College

The Dangerous Samaritans: How We Unintentionally Injure the Poor

Michael Bauman

Michael Bauman is a professor of theology and culture and director of Christian Studies at Hillsdale College. He is also a lecturer and tutor in Renaissance literature and theology as well as associate dean at the Centre for Medieval and Renaissance Studies in Oxford. He has been book review editor for *The Journal of the Evangelical Theological Society* for seven years.

Formerly an editorial assistant at *Newsweek,* a pastor, chairman of the general education program at Northeastern Bible College, and an associate professor of religion at Fordham University, Dr. Bauman is the author of more than thirty articles and eight books, including *Pilgrim Theology: Taking the Path of Theological Discovery* (Zondervan, 1992), *Roundtable: Conversations with European Theologians* (Baker, 1990), *A Scripture Index to John Milton's* De Doctrina Christiana (MRTS, 1989), *Milton's Arianism* (Verlag Peter Lang, 1987), and editor or co-editor of *Are You Politically Correct? Debating America's Cultural Standards* (Prometheus, 1993), *The Best of the Manion Forum* (MRUP, 1991), and Hillsdale's *Christian Vision* series.

We think we are doing the right thing.

We think that if we pass laws to raise their wages and lower their rent, if we give generously to help support mothers without husbands and children without fathers, we can aid the poor in their flight from poverty and alleviate much of their distress.

We are wrong.

We forget that good intentions are not enough and that massive government programs carry unintended consequences. We forget that aiming is not hitting and that meaning well is not necessarily doing well.

Minimum Wage Laws

First, we think that if we pass laws mandating higher wages for the lowest paid workers, we can increase their income. We forget that the lowest paid workers are normally those with the least skill and experience and that in the marketplace they are the least desirable of all workers. By artificially elevating their wages, we make them even more undesirable, and we make it increasingly unlikely that they can get or keep a job. We forget that a wage is not merely a selling price for a worker; it is a purchase price for an employer. So we pass laws preventing the least desirable workers from selling their services at a price their prospective employers can afford to pay.

We also forget that all workers work not merely for their employer, but for the consumer, and that consumers wisely try to make the most of their money. Nevertheless, due to our desire to be moral and compassionate people, we pass laws requiring employers to pay higher wages to their least desirable workers while, as good stewards of the resources God has given us, we choose not to buy the over-priced products of those who do as the law demands. We put them out of business, which creates more unemployed workers and more poor, whom we then foolishly try to help with more minimum wage laws.

Imagine if we decided to prop up the profits of the weakest auto manufacturer in Detroit by passing a law that put a minimum price of $25,000 on each vehicle it sold. This would dramatically increase the profits it enjoys from every sale. But, despite our good intentions, indeed because of our good intentions, that manufacturer would soon go out of business. No matter how much consumers might want to "buy American," very few can or will pay $25,000 for automobiles comparable to those available elsewhere at half the legally mandated price. The same principle holds true when that which is being sold is not an automobile but an unskilled employee's over-priced labor. When minimum wage laws are in effect, the choice often is not between the legally mandated wage and some other wage, but between the legally mandated wage and no wage at all.

To such well-intentioned but harmful legislative conniving, no thinking Christian or other religious believer ought to consent. If we want to make the marketplace more moral, or if we want to be agents of effective compassion, minimum wage laws are not the answer. Instead, as Hillsdale College economist Charles Van Eaton argues, we ought to encourage more entrepreneurship. Look at the examples of the late Dave Thomas and Ray Kroc. Far more than any government program ever has or could, the businesses they established—McDonald's and Wendy's—aid the poor as consumers by providing affordable, enjoyable meals outside the home—a privilege once reserved for the wealthy. They aid the poor as workers by providing all-important entry level jobs that allow experience to be gained and critical marketplace lessons to be learned—from the importance of appearance, punctuality, deference, teamwork, integrity and dependability to more sophisticated management and public relations skills. They also offer a modest wage to boot.

Entrepreneurs like Kroc and Thomas understand that you cannot climb the ladder of success without first getting on the ladder. They invite the poor to step onto the first rung and begin climbing. Hundreds of thousands of people prosper in precisely this way, all without spending even one tax dollar. Quite the opposite: These novice workers, as they rise from poverty, actually pay into the public coffers. At one time or another, nearly one-eighth of the entire American work force has been employed by the fast food industry, and of that number, many previously poor workers have gone on to better jobs and a level of prosperity that otherwise would have remained unattainable. Some even have gone on to own fast food franchises themselves, which help others stepping onto that first rung.

Housing Laws

Second, we think that if we pass laws holding down the costs of urban housing, we can aid the poor by making more inexpensive lodgings available to them, perhaps diminishing homelessness in the process. We forget that a purchase price for a renter is a selling price for a landlord. The more attractive a price is for the one, the less attractive it is for the other. When landlords are forced to reduce their rents in the face of burgeoning tax and maintenance costs, those landlords wisely decide to allocate their investments in other ways. For example, when rent control ceilings make it unprofitable for landlords to rent their apartments, they often sell those apartments as condominiums and thus escape real estate taxes and the high cost of upkeep. Because the supply of condominiums increases, their selling price tends to go down, thereby aiding wealthier urban dwellers, the only ones who can afford to purchase them. Meanwhile, the price of the apartments still remaining on the market rises because their supply has shrunk.

In order to prevent this from happening, we occasionally pass laws prohibiting landlords from taking recourse to condominium conversion. This legislative ban proves counter-productive because it often means: (1) that landlords seek additional payments under the table from their renters, thus making life more difficult for the poor, who can scarcely afford the extra cost; (2) that landlords defer needed maintenance on their decaying buildings, again making life more difficult for the poor; and (3) that landlords get out of the housing business altogether, tear down their apartments and build parking lots—low-maintenance, high-yield investments that serve only those wealthy enough to afford the high cost of owning, operating, and insuring an automobile in an urban location.

We forget that, human nature being what it is, people respond to incentives. Instead of passing rent control laws in order to aid our poorer neighbors, we ought to give substantially reduced public utility rates and increased tax breaks to those who establish urban rental housing. This would make such housing more plentiful, more affordable, and more comfortable. In short, if we do anything at all by means of the state, we should do all we can to promote the supply side of the supply and demand equation. The greater the incentives for property owners, the better it is for land-lords. The better it is for landlords, the greater the supply of apartments. The greater the supply of apartments, the lower the price. The lower the price, the better it is for the poor. And the subsequent increase in urban rental units not only results in lower rental prices for renters but also pro-vides more jobs for those who construct apartment buildings, as well as for those who service and maintain them.

Welfare Laws

Third, we think that by transferring money as gener-ously as we can afford to the mothers of illegitimate children, we can soften the pains of youngsters without fathers and of mothers without husbands. We forget what insurance com-panies call the "moral hazard," which is insuring against a disaster in a way that encourages it to happen.

Insurance companies know all too well that people re-spond to incentives. If the fire insurance policy on a foun-dering business pays more money to the owner than the owner can get from operating it, that business may go up in smoke—literally. Likewise, if a life insurance policy pays off so lucratively that the insured's beneficiaries are better off if the insured is dead, death sometimes results. If medical in-surance covers too great a portion of medical expenses, peo-ple tend to apply for treatment of illnesses that are hardly illnesses at all, thus tying up doctors and hospitals with rela-tively trivial cases. In other words, when we reach the point of moral hazard, fire insurance causes fires, life insurance causes death, and medical insurance causes illness. Not sur-prisingly, insurance companies always try very hard to avoid the moral hazard inherent in insurance.

We don't.

In our rush to do well for households without a male bread-winner, we forget that welfare is poverty insurance, and, as a result, we actually help cause the problem we intend to alleviate. By making illegitimate children a credential for increased financial support, we make certain more illegiti-mate children are born. And we do so in a particularly amoral way. As Patty Newman, author of *Pass the Poverty, Please,* relates: "Can you imagine my shock when I went into a welfare department and said, 'Do you mean to tell me that a woman can come in here every nine months and begin to get checks for another illegitimate child?' The welfare man said, 'Oh, no, Mrs. Newman, she has to claim a different man as father every time or else she doesn't get the money.'"

Tragically, the more illegitimate children a woman has, the more deeply she becomes mired in poverty, and the less likely it is that she can ever extricate herself, despite the money she is given by government. Welfare is, in the words of Robert Rector, an incentive program from Hell. As long as we pay the poor to continue doing the very things that help make them poor in the first place, poor they shall remain.

Put differently, what you pay for is what you get. Because single motherhood is what we decide to pay for with our tax money, more single mothers are what we get. The tragic fact is that in the last decade or so in America, more than 80 percent of the children born in the urban black underclass were born out of wedlock and without an adult male to accept any financial responsibility for them. Of course, rising illegitimacy is neither a distinctively black nor a distinctively American problem. Sweden, for example, which subsidizes its unwed mothers even more generously than we do, has the highest rate of illegitimacy in the world. Just as when you tax something, you get less of it, when you subsidize it, you get more. Today, we are subsidizing immoral behavior on a grand scale. As a result, immoral behavior flourishes all around us, while those who practice it are harmed. This is no way to bring morality to the marketplace.

Another unintended consequence of our efforts to aid single mothers and their children is that low income husbands are made extraneous. Welfare actually drives them from the home. The average total relief package for a single mother with three children is more than $19,000 a year—tax free. By comparison, a traditional two-parent family of four with a higher income, of say $22,500, has only about $18,000 left after taxes. Poor women might be poor, but they are not stupid. Neither are poor young men, many of whom quickly realize that by their own efforts and means they are unable to provide as well for their families as does their rich Uncle Sam in Washington.

Uncle Sam is exceedingly tough competition. Too many mothers decide not to marry the fathers of their children; they marry welfare instead. Thus government makes cuckolds of millions of American men. As George Gilder, author of *Wealth and Poverty,* once observed, the modern welfare state has persuaded poor fathers that they are dispensable. They believe it; so do the mothers of their children. By means of our so-called compassion and generosity, we send the signal to many thousands of women—especially poor, young women eager to get out of their parents' homes and away from their parents' control—that men are most useful as procreators, not as providers.

To men—especially poor, young men who tend to live more for the moment than the future—that same signal has a different but equally devastating effect. We teach them that, if they want it, sex is a game they can play for free. No longer is there heavy pressure upon them to face up to the consequences of sex outside marriage. No longer do they feel compelled to work long hours at difficult jobs in order to provide food, clothing, and shelter for the new lives they create or for the financially dependent women who help create them. That tab, young men quickly learn, will be picked up by the government, provided that they do nothing to help the mother or to assume responsibility.

With no compelling need to channel time and energy into acquiring useful skills and into applying those skills profitably in the marketplace, increasing numbers of young men simply take to the streets, where life gets boring and then gets much worse. Without work there is no economic prosperity, and without incentives there is no work.

In our misguided efforts to help those lying in the ditch of poverty—to be good Samaritans—we forget that whatever undermines traditional family values, traditional family roles, and traditional family ties undermines society itself. To such moral and social degeneration, we ought never to subscribe. Our first priority, as well as the first priority of any government program of poverty relief, ought to be to stabilize traditional family roles and responsibilities.

False Charity

Fourth, by giving money to the poor, we think we simply are aiding and comforting the unfortunate in their time of difficulty. We forget that giving good gifts is an exceedingly difficult endeavor and that poverty is not always itself the problem; it is often the symptom of another prior problem. That is, if poverty (the lack of money) really were what ails the poor, supplying vast amounts of money surely would alleviate it. But after thirty years of Great Society-style "War on Poverty" welfare programs—programs that have transferred (in 1990 dollars) more than $3.6 trillion to the poor—poverty is still winning. We ought to think about that for a minute: In the last thirty years, we gave a million dollars to America's poor nearly four million times over, yet all the while poverty got worse. If the money earmarked for poverty relief in this year's federal budget alone were given to the poor directly, we would have enough funds to raise every man, woman, and child in America above the poverty line and have a cool $60 billion left over to celebrate our victory.

Poverty is not primarily a lack of money; it is a lack of something else. While we throw record amounts of money at the problem, we forget that of the many reasons why people are poor, relatively few truly lie outside their own control or require external remedy. And because of this lapse, we fail to convince the poor that the surest way to get ahead in modern America is precisely the way their forefathers did it: get a good education (which includes a mastery of English and math); work hard; save money; and invest.

Instead, we tell the poor that in order to get ahead they need to demand more money from government, as if financial improvement were a public entitlement, not a private achievement, and as if the modern poor were somehow incapable of succeeding by using the same means countless other Americans have used in the past. Then, apparently in an effort to waive the responsibility of the poor to make their own lives better and to lighten the "burden" such responsibility entails, we tell the poor that they are poor because the wealthy oppress them. In other words, we teach the poor to blame their poverty on prejudice.

In a perverse sort of way, of course, we are right. Indeed, prejudice does lead to poverty, though not always in the way we expect or explain. We convince the poor that the prosperous prosper only at someone else's expense and usually by deceit and because of greed. Not only are such insulting generalizations untrue and instances of bearing false witness against our neighbors, they are crippling to the poor. If the poor believe that most wealthy people are exploiters and thieves who squash other people into poverty for personal gain, they will not be likely to climb the ladder of economic success. They will remain poor because they do not respect or try to emulate the achievement of others and because they are blind to the real path the wealthy typically take to success—hard work, diligence, ingenuity, sacrifice, and postponed gratification.

At our hands, then, the poor are convinced that they are poor primarily because of reasons they cannot change and over which they have no control. We teach the poor to be prejudiced themselves—prejudiced against the prosperous. That prejudice proves morally and economically debilitating. We blame poverty on prejudice and then promote prejudice among the poor. It is no wonder that many of the poor simply give up.

We forget not only that ideas have consequences, but that bad ideas have bad consequences. We forget that real poverty is at least as much a state of mind as it is a state of income. We also forget to tie our charity more securely to the sincere efforts of the recipient. We mistakenly decide to give aid to all the poor rather than to the deserving and industrious poor, that is, to those who are poor through no fault of their own, or whose escape from poverty can never be accomplished by their own efforts. In doing so, we ignore St. Paul's prudent scriptural principle: "If a man will not work, he shall not eat." (2 Thess. 3:10, NIV).

We should remember that Christian love does not squander either its resources or itself in reckless disregard of individual character and actions. By obliterating the distinction between the deserving and the undeserving poor, we run contrary to the will and practice of God, who treats the undeserving poor as objects not of mercy but of wrath. In other words, we forget that real love helps those who cannot help themselves, and that it refuses to subsidize sluggardliness or indolence by doing for others what they can and ought to do for themselves. Christian love operates upon the premise that the defeat of poverty is a joint effort, or common endeavor, between the "haves" and the "have nots," not a unilateral thrust by the "haves" only. The recipients of Christian charity ought to be either diligent workers or else unable. The undeserving poor must get nothing from their Christian neighbors but exhortation. To subsidize them is to make way for dependency and indolence, not prosperity. Worse, it is to do them moral injury.

As long as we fail to distinguish between the deserving and the undeserving poor, we teach others that poverty is an entitlement and a credential and that the blessings of life and labor are available for the asking or for the demanding, regardless of one's contribution. People who believe this perverse message can never grow to be productive citizens. They are doomed to be mere wards of the state, forever impoverished in spiritual as well as material terms.

True Charity

The welfare state not only tempts its recipients with nearly irresistible perverse incentives, it seduces those outside it as well, especially those who seek to administer it and those who pay for it. The German economist Wilhelm Röpke wrote:

> To expand the welfare state is not only easy, but it is also one of the surest means for the demagogue to win votes and political influence, and it is for all of us the most ordinary temptation to gain a reputation for generosity and kindness. The welfare state is the favorite playground of a cheap sort

of moralism that only thoughtlessness shields from exposure. . . . Cheap moralism is anything but moral.

We appear to be virtuous when we really are rather lazy "do-gooders" content to let the welfare bureaucrats handle all that "poverty unpleasantness" for us. We say, "Ah, but at least we feel good about ourselves." More frequently than we care to admit, our poverty programs are thinly veiled efforts to enhance our self-esteem and to assuage our consciences by means of state programs. To imagine that by such shallow and self-gratifying efforts we can eliminate human poverty is shameless hubris, not charity and grace. The size of the federal budget is by no means an indicator of Christian compassion.

On many fronts and in many ways, our poverty programs fail to reduce poverty. What is worse, they tend to injure the very persons they are designed to aid. Because we fail to incarnate our good intentions with effective, well-conceived public policy, and because, in the words of George Mason University economist Walter Williams, we fail to realize that truly compassionate public policy requires dispassionate analysis. And because we choose to think with our hearts instead of our brains, much of the blame is ours. We should realize that real prosperity is created from the bottom up, not from the government down. Wealth must be created, not redistributed.

And if we think the outcomes of the marketplace are not up to our moral standards, we must never again forget that true charity does not lead to the welfare state. The Kingdom of God and the Great Society lie in opposite directions. We can help the poor, but we must do so as good, rather than dangerous, Samaritans. Our first tasks are:

1. *Put welfare programs in the hands of contributors, not recipients or bureaucrats.* Welfare recipients and bureaucrats who profit from the enlargement of the welfare state actually have banded together to form lobbies on Capitol Hill, hectoring legislators to redistribute even greater shares of other people's money and to do so as if access to this money were their God-given right. Gone is the notion that welfare is a

form of charity or that escape from it is the responsibility of the poor. Welfare is now viewed as an entitlement. But if the poor have a natural right to the money earned by others, then charity, which is voluntary giving, is impossible.

Rather than assigning control of welfare payments to the poor or to bureaucrats, we ought to give increased discretion over charitable contributions to the donors themselves. This is done best by giving tax credits (not income deductions) for all documentable charity of, say, up to 40 percent of one's total tax bill. This has the effect of making government charity compete for our philanthropy dollars, which will tend to make government programs more effective, more efficient, and less expensive.

2. *Redefine poverty.* Nearly 40 percent of those the U.S. government defines as "poor" own their own homes—homes that have more living space than that enjoyed by most middle class Europeans. "Poor" ought to retain its earlier definition: the lack of food, shelter, or clothing. And while we are engaged in the task of redefining, we ought to remind ourselves that the definition of compassion is not increased control of private income by government.

3. *Re-educate the politicians and the poor.* We must remind politicians that to promote the general welfare is not the same as promoting welfare generally. They ought to think not in terms of dollars but in terms of morality and responsibility and always keep in mind that welfare payments can prove psychologically addictive and debilitating both to those who receive them and to those who provide them. They also must remember that pride in including more and more people on the dole is misplaced; they are not political saints but political pushers when they encourage government paternalism.

As for the poor, we must remind them that it is not a shame to be poor; it is a shame to be lazy and unproductive. Generations of Americans knew how to be something many of today's poor do not: how to be both poor and proud—proud of their modest but hard-won earnings, and of the natural human dignity that does not depend upon a bank account. Nor should the poor shun honest wages for honest work. Too many of today's poor are not proud, they are arrogant. They consider themselves too good to do the menial labor one must perform in order to begin climbing the ladder of success. Yet they are not too proud to take welfare; they are too proud only to flip hamburgers. We must remind them that they have to begin at the bottom and do the jobs no one else wants to do if they wish to stop being poor.

4. *No perfect solutions are possible.* Poverty cannot be eradicated; it can only be ameliorated. But at least we can keep it from getting much worse and prevent ourselves from making it so. We must not expend scarce resources trying to solve the insoluble. The good news is that there is a lot we can do, and we do not need government help to do it.

5. *Abundance can be wrenched from scarcity only by following the Golden Rule of doing unto others as we would have them do unto us.* In a world of scarcity, the important question is not how poverty is gotten but how wealth is achieved. It is easy to become poor and to stay that way. But to become rich, we must learn to supply our neighbors' wants and needs. By being good Samaritans in the marketplace, we help not only ourselves but all mankind.

Stewardship in a Free Society

E. Calvin Beisner

Cal Beisner is an author, editor, and speaker on the Christian worldview and the application of Christian theology and ethics to economics, political science, and public policy, and on reasons for faith. A visiting lecturer in interdisciplinary studies at Covenant College, he is the author of eight books and over one hundred published articles and reviews. He also has been a contributing editor to *The Marketplace Bible*, a joint project of Intervarsity Christian Fellowship and Thomas Nelson Publishers and a contributor to six other books.

His own latest books are *Answers For Atheists, Agnostics and Other Thoughtful Skeptics—Dialogues About Christian Faith and Life* (Crossway Books, 1993); *Prospects for Growth: A Biblical View of Population, Resources and the Future* (Crossway Books, 1990), and *Prosperity and Poverty: The Compassionate Use of Resources in a World of Scarcity* (Crossway Books, 1988).

Conservatives, Russell Kirk often pointed out, have a habit of taking definitions seriously. We should. For many misunderstandings stem from wrong definitions, and from misunderstandings arise mistakes. So I launch this discussion of stewardship in a free market with some definitions—of *stewardship*, of *freedom*, and of *markets*.

Stewardship

Our first key term, *stewardship*, has origins and meanings, both humble and exalted. The English word *steward* derives from the Anglo-Saxon *stîweard* or *stigeweard*—literally, the ward, or keeper, of a sty for cattle and pigs. It denotes, as Webster tells us, a man entrusted with the management of the household or estate of another, one employed to manage the domestic affairs, superintend the servants, collect the rents or income, or keep the accounts of the estate's owner. The position, duties, or services entrusted to such a man are his *stewardship*. Such are the meanings, too, of the words translated *steward* and *stewardship* in the New Testament: the verb *oikonomé*— means to manage as a house-steward, to order, to regulate; the noun *oikonomía*—the origin of our word *economy*—denotes the management of a household or family, hence, thrift; and the noun *oikonómos* denotes one who manages a household. All of these Greek words, by the way, find their roots in the words for *house* and *law* or *rule*.

While the steward's position is humble, it demands integrity. One naturally hopes, therefore, to find honest men for stewards. Such a man did Shakespeare's surprised Timon of Athens, having despaired of finding anyone honest in this fallen world, declare Flavius, his steward, to be:

> Had I a steward
> So true, so just, and now so comfortable?
> It almost turns my dangerous nature mild.
> Let me behold thy face. . . .
> Forgive my general and exceptless rashness,
> You perpetual-sober gods! I do proclaim
> One honest man. Mistake me not—but one!
> No more, I pray—and he's a steward.
> How fain would I have hated all mankind!
> And thou redeem'st thyself. But all save thee
> I fell with curses.

To such a man one may entrust much. So said Jesus: "Who then is that faithful and wise steward, whom his master will make ruler over his household, to give them their portion of food in due season? Blessed is that servant whom his master will find so doing when he comes. Truly, I say to you that he will make him ruler over all that he has" (Luke 12:42–44). For, as He said on another occasion, "He who is faithful in what is least is faithful also in much; and he who is unjust in what is least is unjust also in much" (Luke 16:10).

Indeed. It is fitting, then, that a word that first denoted the ward of a pig sty should later come to denote a royal officer—even, in the person of the *Lord High Steward,* the most powerful man in the realm save the king himself. To be a steward is an honor.

It is also an honor easily abused. Take, for example, another steward of whom Jesus spoke, in that strange Parable of the Unjust Steward:

> There was a certain rich man who had a steward, and an accusation was brought to him that this man was wasting his goods. So he called him and said to him, "What is this I hear about you? Give an account of your stewardship, for you can no longer be steward." Then the steward said within himself, "What shall I do? For my master is taking the stewardship away from me. I cannot dig; I am ashamed to beg. I have resolved what to do, that when I am put out of the steward- ship, they may receive me into their houses." So he called every one of his master's debtors to him, and said to the first, "How much do you owe my master?" And he said, "A hun- dred measures of oil." So he said to him, "Take your bill, and sit down quickly and write fifty." Then he said to another, "And how much do you owe?" So he said, "A hundred mea- sures of wheat." And he said to him, "Take your bill, and write eighty." So the master commended the unjust steward because he had dealt shrewdly. For the sons of this world are more shrewd in their generation than the sons of light. And I say to you, make friends for yourselves by unrighteous mammon, that when you fail, they may receive you into an everlasting home. (Luke 16:1–9)

This man might not have been honest, but he knew how to make friends! Nonetheless, though his master praised him for his shrewdness, he certainly never trusted him again. To be a good steward, then—a faithful and wise steward who will advance in service and authority—one must be not only shrewd but also honest.

Freedom

Our first principal term, *stewardship,* and our second, *freedom,* stand together seemingly in tension. Stewardship in- herently bespeaks accountability; a steward is always answer- able to someone greater than himself. But accountability seems, at first glance, the antithesis of freedom. To be free, we are told in our age—the age of autonomy, Francis Schaeffer dubbed it in *The Great Evangelical Disaster*—means precisely *not* to be accountable. To be free in this sense is to be utterly self-ruled—not merely self-governed (for one may govern under law as well as by law), but self-ruled, *autonomous,* a law (Greek *nómos*) to oneself (Greek *autós*). But such is neither the classical meaning of the term nor the Christian.

The Teutonic root of our English word *free* described a protected member of the community; it distinguished between those who were enslaved to others and those who were their own masters. Similarly, the Latin *liber* (from which the English *liberty* derives), and the Greek *eleutheros* both referred to the same distinction between slave and freeman. Properly understood, then, *freedom* is neither political self-determination nor the ability to do whatever one chooses without cost— that is, the absence of natural and economic restraints on human action—nor the absence of moral restraints and their enforcement, but exemption from arbitrary coercion by others.

The Christian vision of freedom accepts but goes beyond this classical vision. St. Augustine insisted that true freedom is something deeper than mere immunity to forced servitude to others, something rooted in the very nature of the free man. It is one's ability to live as he was created to live, to walk in righteousness according to the law of God, not in licentious rebellion against that law.

For Augustine, to defy the divine law is to destroy freedom. Why? We can understand Augustine's argument best by contrasting—as he does—his understanding of freedom with his understanding of slavery. Noting that the Latin word *servus,* which we translate "slave," comes from the word *servare,* "to preserve," Augustine believed that "The origin of the Latin word for slave is supposed to be found in the circumstance that those who by the law of war were liable to be killed were sometimes preserved by their victors, and were hence called servants. And these circumstances"—i.e., that there should be war, and victors, and those preserved from a just death and thus made slaves—"these circumstances," he continued,

> could never have arisen save through sin. For even when we wage a just war, our adversaries must be sinning; and every victory, even though gained by wicked men, is a result of the first judgment of God, who humbles the vanquished either for the sake of removing or of punishing their sins. . . . The prime cause, then, of slavery is sin, which brings man under the dominion of his fellow,—that which does not happen save by the judgment of God, with whom is no unrighteousness, and who knows how to award fit punishments to every variety of offence. But our Master in heaven says, "Every one who doeth sin is the servant of sin" [John 8:34]. And thus there are many wicked masters who have religious men as their slaves, and who are yet themselves in bondage; "for of whom a man is overcome, of the same is he brought in bondage" [2 Peter 2:19].

Augustine does not rest with discussing the superficial slavery of man to man. Why are wicked masters "themselves in bondage"? Because they are brought in bondage by the sin that has overcome them:

> And beyond question it is a happier thing to be the slave of a man than of a lust; for even this very lust of ruling, to mention no others, lays waste men's hearts with the most ruthless dominion.[1]

For Augustine, to sin is to be at war with God and His law. Such a war no man can win. But though the just reward of sin, as of treason, is death (Romans 6:23), God, in His mercy, preserves rebellious sinners. Yet their very preservation is servitude—slavery to sin, until at last they repent and are set free from it.

In all of this Augustine follows the lead of Jesus and the Apostle Paul. "Truly, truly, I say to you," said Jesus, "every one who commits sin is a slave to sin." Nonetheless, "if the Son makes you free, you will be free indeed" (John 8:34, 36). Yet it is only by repentance—by dying to oneself, accepting that just sentence against the rebel vanquished in war—that one may follow the Son of God. For "he who does not take his cross and follow me is not worthy of me. He who finds his life will lose it, and he who loses his life for my sake will find it" (Matthew 10:38–39).

St. Paul explains:

> We know that our old self was crucified with him so that the sinful body might be destroyed, and we might no longer be enslaved to sin. For he who has died is freed from sin. But if we have died with Christ, we believe that we shall also live with him. For we know that Christ being raised from the dead will never die again; death no longer has dominion over him. The death he died he died to sin, once for all, but the life he lives he lives to God. So you also must consider yourselves dead to sin [and therefore, in Augustine's line of thought, no longer preserved from death, i.e., no longer enslaved to sin] and alive to God in Christ Jesus.
>
> Let not sin therefore reign in your mortal bodies, to make you obey their passions. Do not yield your members to sin as instruments of wickedness, but yield yourselves to God as men who have been brought from death to life, and your members to God as instruments of righteousness. For sin will have no dominion over you, since you are not under law but under grace.
>
> What then? Are we to sin because we are not under law but under grace? By no means! Do you not know that if you yield yourselves to any one as obedient slaves, you are slaves of the one whom you obey, either of sin, which leads to death, or of obedience, which leads to righteousness? But thanks be to God, that you who were once slaves of sin have become obedient from the heart to the standard of teaching to which you were committed, and, *having been set free from sin, have become slaves of righteousness.* . . .
>
> When you were slaves of sin, you were free in regard to righteousness. . . . But now that you have been set free from sin and have become slaves of God, the return you get is sanctification and its end, eternal life. For the wages of sin is death, but the free gift of God is eternal life in Christ Jesus our Lord. [Romans 6:6–18, 20, 22–23]

The Christian vision of freedom, then, is the restoration of man to proper submission to his Maker. This liberty—not self-indulgence but virtuous self-control under divine law—is the foundation on which a just and peaceable order rests.

The great statesman Edmund Burke, founder of conservatism, understood the links between liberty and virtue, between slavery and vice, between authority and submission and order. "The distinguishing part of our Constitution," he told the voters at Bristol, "is its liberty. To preserve that liberty inviolate seems the particular duty and proper trust of a member of the House of Commons. But the liberty, the only liberty, I mean is a liberty connected with order: that not only exists along with order and virtue, but which cannot exist at all without them."[2] For Burke, "Abstract liberty, like other mere abstractions, is not to be found."[3]

Thus Burke explained in his letter to the Sheriffs of Bristol, "Civil freedom, Gentlemen, is not, as many have endeavored to persuade you, a thing that lies hid in the depth of abstruse science. It is a blessing and a benefit, not an abstract speculation.... The *extreme* of liberty," by which Burke meant the rejection of all moral restraint, "which is its abstract perfection, but its real fault) obtains nowhere, nor ought to obtain anywhere; because extremes, as we all know, in every point which relates either to our duties or satisfactions in life, are destructive both to virtue and enjoyment. Liberty, too, must be limited in order to be possessed." For Burke, despotism is no greater threat to liberty than libertinism, the frame of mind of those by whom "every government is called tyranny and usurpation which is not formed on their fancies. In this manner the stirrers up of this contention, not satisfied with distracting our dependencies and filling them with blood and slaughter, are corrupting our understandings: They are endeavoring to tear up, along with practical liberty, all the foundations of human society, all equity and justice, religion and order."[4]

Properly understood, then, stewardship—with its accountability and its submission to authority—stands not opposed to freedom but complementary to it. The two support each other. True freedom is the liberty to do what is right, not the license to do whatever we wish; and faithfulness to what is right is the heart of stewardship.

How do these stand, however, in relation to the market? What do we mean by stewardship in a free *market*?

The Market

The Anglo-Saxon word *market* derives from the Latin *mercatus,* trade or market place, which in turn is the past participle of *mercari,* to trade.

When, in economics, we speak of "the market," we refer not simply to the fact that trade occurs, but to the fact that trade and traders *define* and *determine* what occurs. Those who do the trading make their own decisions; they are not commanded by others. Thus the *market economy* (and remember that *economy* is *oikonomía,* which we also translate as *stewardship*) contrasts with a *controlled* or *planned* or *managed* economy. In the latter, force or the threat of force determines what trades occur and under what conditions, and it is the use or threat of force for any purpose other than to keep the peace and execute justice—i.e., the use of arbitrary force—that violates freedom.

This is, as I have said, a concept simple in principle but exceedingly complex in practice. For in protecting the freedom of the many, it substitutes for the conscious and general direction of one or a few people the apparent indirection of millions. And this, to some, appears mere anarchy. Such people cannot tolerate the unpredictability of the market; they feel insecure because of it, and so they yearn for someone to bring order out of this chaos—perhaps they yearn to do so themselves! And in direct proportion as they think themselves fit for the task, just so far are they unworthy of the trust. Unworthy, because they are blind to the complexity and variety of human aspirations and talents; because they are blind to the impossibility of sustaining true freedom among those whose lives must be directed, in their most routine and daily elements, by others; and because they are blind to their own sinfulness which must, if they are entrusted with such enormous power over others, necessarily lead to their abusing them. "Power tends to corrupt," wrote Lord Acton, "and absolute power corrupts absolutely. Great men are almost always bad men, even when they exercise influence and not authority; still more when you superadd the tendency or the certainty of corruption by authority."[5]

Our observations on stewardship and freedom should instantly correct the mistaken notion that a free market is anarchy or chaos. It is the farthest thing from both. For in the truly *free* market, choices uncoerced find guidance in virtue, and stewards know they must give account to their Master in Heaven.

A free market, in short, can function only so long as, and only so well as, it remains truly free and does not degenerate into licentiousness. In Burke's words, "Among a people generally corrupt, liberty cannot long exist."[6]

The Exercise of Stewardship in a Free Market

So much for definitions. What do these things mean in practice? Much more could be said than time permits today. I focus, then, on three matters: (1) what stewardship in a free market must not mean; (2) the spheres of stewardship; and (3) the virtues on which effective stewardship must stand.

What Stewardship in a Free Market Must Not Mean

Economist Paul Heyne has said that he cringes to hear people equate economics with stewardship—despite the etymology of our word *economics*. He rejects the notion that any person or group of persons is even capable of stewarding— that is, managing, directing, guiding, supervising—the whole great fabric of trade that we call the market. This fabric not only is too vast and too intricate to be known adequately for such central guidance, but also changes too quickly.

Heyne is right. It is the depth of folly to think, and the height of hubris to try, either to comprehend or to control such an arrangement. But that it is inappropriate to speak of a stewardship of the whole does not imply the same of the parts. True, no one can manage the entire market, or even a significantly large part of it, and disaster follows every attempt. But everyone in the market can—and, if the market is to remain free, must—manage, or steward, himself and his responsibilities. And so we turn to the spheres of stewardship.

Spheres of Stewardship

Stewardship properly begins in the narrowest circles. A man must govern himself before he can be trusted to govern others. He must govern and provide for his own family before he can for a larger company. He must conduct his own business well before he endeavors to conduct the business of a whole community. Viewed thus, it is clear that in the market, and in the free society as a whole, power must flow from the bottom up, not from the top down; it must expand into ever-widening, and ever-weakening, circles. The greatest power—because the most focused—should be local, not national.

The corollary of this is that each individual must be satisfied to leave the great mass of affairs outside his control. More, he must be satisfied to know that no human being, and no group of human beings, controls the great and wide affairs of men. He must trust, in other words, not to human design but to divine providence for the ordering of the market, and of the whole civil social order, to his and every other person's benefit.

This, not impersonal fate, was what Adam Smith meant by the "invisible hand" that guides people to serve their fellow men through no conscious intent of their own but rather through the pursuit of their own legitimate interests. In the best known of his uses of that famous phrase, in his *Inquiry into the Nature and Causes of the Wealth of Nations,* Smith wrote:

> As every individual, therefore, endeavours as much as he can both to employ his capital in the support of domestic industry, and so to direct that industry that its produce may be of the greatest value; every individual necessarily labours to render the annual revenue of the society as great as he can. He generally, indeed, neither intends to promote the public interest, nor knows how much he is promoting it. By preferring the support of domestic to that of foreign industry, he intends only his own security; and by directing that industry in such a manner as its produce may be of the greatest value, he intends only his own gain, and he is in this, as in many

other cases, led by an invisible hand to promote an end which was no part of his intention. Nor is it always the worse for the society that it was no part of it. By pursuing his own interest he frequently promotes that of the society more effectually than when he really intends to promote it.[7]

By taking this in isolation from Smith's underlying philosophy—and here we recall that Smith was not an economist by profession, but a professor of moral philosophy—we easily fail to see the theological basis of Smith's thought. In an earlier use of the phrase, in *The Theory of Moral Sentiments*, Smith had in mind the providence of God.[8] Was this a mere rhetorical device for him, or did it represent a conscious belief in the superintending, loving activity of a personal God? Was it more akin to the philosophy of the Stoics and deists, or to St. Paul's confident assertion "that all things work together for good to those who love God, to those who are the called according to His purpose" (Romans 8:28)? I believe a careful reading of *The Theory of Moral Sentiments* leads to the latter conclusion, and it does so in a manner that calls to mind our recognition that social responsibility should follow the natural, concentric, and widening circles formed by the individual, the family, the community, and the nation. "Every man," wrote Smith,

> ... is first and principally recommended to his own care; and every man is certainly, in every respect, fitter and abler to take care of himself than of any other person. Every man feels his own pleasures and his own pains more sensibly than those of other people....
>
> After himself, the members of his own family, those who usually live in the same house with him, his parents, his children, his brothers and sisters, are naturally the objects of his warmest affections. They are naturally and usually the persons upon whose happiness or misery his conduct must have the greatest influence. He is more habituated to sympathize with them. He knows better how every thing is likely to affect them, and his sympathy with them is more precise and determinate, than it can be with the greater part of other people.... (VI.ii.i.1–2.)

The same principles that direct the order in which individuals are recommended to our beneficence, direct that likewise in which societies are recommended to it. Those to which it is, or may be of most importance, are first and principally recommended to it. (VI.ii.ii.1.)

In saying these things, Smith did but follow in the footsteps of St. Augustine, who, in *The City of God,* wrote of the peaceable order of the just community,

... this is the order of this concord, that a man, in the first place, injure no one, and, in the second, do good to every one he can reach. Primarily, therefore, his own household are his care, for the law of nature and of society gives him readier access to them and greater opportunity of serving them. And hence the apostle says, "Now, if any provide not for his own, and specially for those of his own house, he hath denied the faith, and is worse than an infidel" [1 Timothy 5:8].[9]

While, then, the circles of our care grow ever wider, they also grow ever dimmer because of our own limitations of knowledge, of understanding, and of foresight. Care for ourselves and our families, our friends and close communities, Smith recognized, is a matter for our conscious intention:

[But the] administration of the great system of the universe, however, the care of the universal happiness of all rational and sensible beings, is the business of God and not of man. To man is allotted a much humbler department, but one much more suitable to the weakness of his powers, and to the narrowness of his comprehension; the care of his own happiness, of that of his family, his friends, his country: that he is occupied in contemplating the more sublime, can never be an excuse for his neglecting the more humble department.... (*Theory of Moral Sentiments,* VI.ii.ii.6.)

For Smith, the providence of God was not the impersonal stuff of deism but the "benevolence and wisdom" of God. This providence, he said, was "certainly of all the objects of human contemplation by far the most sublime" (VI.ii.ii.5). It is a "wisdom that directs all the events of human life" and against which the wise man never complains, recognizing in it provision for the good of all (VII.ii.i.20).

The Virtues on Which Effective Stewardship Must Stand

Although commonly misunderstood by those who have not read him, Smith never intended his doctrine of the invisible hand to be used as a justification of selfishness. Echoing St. Paul, he believed

> that as the world was governed by the all-ruling providence of a wise, powerful, and good God, every single event ought to be regarded as making a necessary part of the plan of the universe, and as tending to promote the general order and happiness of the whole: that the vices and follies of mankind, therefore, made as necessary a part of this plan as their wisdom or their virtue; and by that eternal art which reduces good from ill, were made to tend equally to the prosperity and perfection of the great system of nature. No speculation of this kind, however, how deeply so ever it might be rooted in the mind, could diminish our natural abhorrence for vice, whose immediate effects are so destructive, and whose remote ones are too distant to be traced by the imagination (I.ii.iii.4).

Far from justifying selfishness, Smith condemned it, holding that the properly formed conscience could approve of nothing less than self-denial for the sake of others:

> And hence it is, that to feel much for others and little for ourselves, that to restrain our selfish, and to indulge our benevolent affections, constitutes the perfection of human nature; and can alone produce among mankind that harmony of sentiments and passions in which consists their whole grace and propriety. As to love our neighbour as we love ourselves is the great law of Christianity, so it is the great precept of nature to love ourselves only as we love our neighbour, or what comes to the same thing, as our neighbour is capable of loving us. (I.i.v.5)

Smith recognized, as did Burke, that order in the commonwealth requires order in the soul; that freedom under divine providence rests on virtue. And so we conclude with a brief consideration of four principal virtues necessary for the flourishing of stewardship in a free market: justice, love, prudence, and humility.

Justice and Love. The root of the free society is justice—not the highest, but the most fundamental of the virtues, the soil in which the other virtues, their roots firmly planted, can risk the ascent of otherwise precarious heights. One can afford the risks of generosity when his property is protected from theft; he can hazard the vulnerability of love when justice prevails about him. For justice, while it does not, like love, compel us to sacrifice ourselves for others, it does—by requiring that we render to each his due—forbid us to sacrifice others for ourselves.

Justice therefore is, as Smith wrote, "the main pillar that upholds the whole edifice [of society]. If it is removed, the great, the immense fabric of human society ... must in a moment crumble into atoms. In order to enforce the observation of justice, therefore, nature has implanted in the human breast that consciousness of ill desert, those terrors of merited punishment, which attend upon its violation, as the great safeguards of the association of mankind, to protect the weak, to curb the violent, and to chastise the guilty" (*Theory of Moral Sentiments,* II.ii.iii.4).

Justice requires that we do no one harm. This is not so noble a sentiment as that we should do good to all—the requirement of love—but without it, all striving after love would be folly.

If justice is the foundation of the free society, love is its loftiest adornment. The society that would subsist on a level higher than what is essential to security, peace, and order, must be driven by love, for no one can rise to his highest potential, whether mentally, morally, or materially, without the aid of others. "All the members of human society," Smith wrote, "stand in need of each others['] assistance.... Where the necessary assistance is reciprocally afforded from love, from gratitude, from friendship, and esteem, the society flourishes and is happy. All the different members of it are bound together by the agreeable bands of love and affection, and are, as it were, drawn to one common centre of mutual good offices" (*Theory of Moral Sentiments,* II.ii.iii.1).

While justice renders to each his due, love graciously bestows benefits to those who have no claim on them. "By this we know love," wrote the Apostle John, "that he laid down his life for us; and we ought to lay down our lives for the brethren. But if any one has the world's goods and sees his brother in need, yet closes his heart against him, how does God's love abide in him? Little children, let us not love in word or speech but in deed and in truth" (1 John 3:16–18).

Prudence and Humility. As justice and love go hand in hand, so also do prudence and humility, and indeed even justice and love cannot properly be effected apart from these more modest virtues.

What is prudence? It is the ability to foresee the consequences of our choices and actions, to recognize how they will affect not only ourselves and those nearest us in time and relation but also those much farther away. And what is humility? It is that modesty that recognizes limits to our minds' capacities and so forbears to exert our own ideas to rule over everyone else's. After all, the mere intent to love is by itself not enough; we must "not love in word or speech but in deed and in truth." Hell is, after all, paved with good intentions, its flagstones laid by people who, motivated by compassion but lacking prudence and humility, have harmed those they wished to help.

Many speak of justice and compassion in America today as necessary components of stewardship, both personal and public. But—not meaning to denigrate justice and love in any way—when hubris entices us to encompass ever-expanding spheres of life in the benign schemes of the omnipotent state, one thinks immediately of the welfare system whose inevitable failure we already experience, and of the drive toward a national health care policy whose failure we will be spared only if it is never attempted. When hubris drives us toward such precipices, the need of the hour becomes restraint. Perhaps a revival of prudence and humility would do more to improve stewardship in a free market than any amount of attention to the loftier virtues of justice and love. So suggested F. A. Hayek in his Nobel lecture, "The Pretense of Knowledge":

The recognition of the insuperable limits to his knowledge ought indeed to teach the student of society a lesson of humility that should keep him from becoming an accomplice in man's fatal striving to control society—a striving that makes him not only a tyrant over his fellows, but may well make him destroy a civilization that no brain has designed, a civilization that has grown from the free efforts of millions of individuals.[10]

We cannot control man more minutely than the broad restrictions of justice written in the divine law without simultaneously exalting some men—the controllers—to godlike status and debasing all others—the controlled—to the status of animals. C. S. Lewis made the same argument in *The Abolition of Man:* " . . . Man's conquest of himself means simply the rule of the Conditioners over the conditioned human material, the world of post-humanity which, some knowingly and some unknowingly, nearly all men in all nations are at present labouring to produce."[11]

St. Augustine commented about God's entrusting to man "dominion over the fish of the sea, and over the birds of the air, and over every creeping thing that creep upon the earth" (Genesis 1:26),

He did not intend that His rational creature, who was made in His image, should have dominion over anything but the irrational creation,—not man over man, but man over the beasts. And hence the righteous men in primitive times were made shepherds of cattle rather than kings of men, God intending thus to teach us what the relative position of the creatures is. . . .[12]

As Arthur Shenfield points out, only capitalism

. . . operates on the basis of respect for free, independent, responsible persons. All other systems in varying degrees treat men as less than this. Socialist systems above all treat men as pawns to be moved about by the authorities, or as children to be given what the rulers decide is good for them, or as serfs or slaves. The rulers begin by boasting about their compassion, which in any case is fraudulent, but after a time they drop this pretense which they find unnecessary for the maintenance of power. In all things they act on the presumption that they know best. Therefore they and their systems are morally stunted. Only the free system, the much assailed capitalism, is morally mature.[13]

To exercise dominion over men and women is to treat them as subhuman. No steward—no ward of the sty—who failed to recognize the difference between the pig and the child who fell into the sty would earn the respect of his master. Neither should the official today who impairs the true freedom with which God endowed mankind, in the name of a false freedom, a false economy, a false justice, or a false love.

"You know," said Jesus, "that the rulers of the Gentiles lord it over them, and their great men exercise authority over them. It shall not be so among you; but whoever would be great among you must be your servant, and whoever would be first among you must be your slave; even as the Son of man came not to be served but to serve, and to give his life as a ransom for many" (Matthew 20:25–28).

Notes

1. St. Augustine, *The City of God,* XIX.xv, *A Select Library of the Nicene and Post-Nicene Fathers of the Christian Church,* Series 1, 14 volumes, edited by Philip Schaff (Grand Rapids: Eerdmans, 1978 reprint), 2:411.

2. "Speech at His Arrival at Bristol," October 13, 1774, *The Writings and Speeches of the Right Honourable Edmund Burke,* 12 volumes (Boston: Little, Brown and Company, 1901), 2:87. Burke's words reflect those of Algernon Sidney, who in defending popular government against absolute monarchy wrote, " . . . if vice and corruption prevail, liberty cannot subsist; but if virtue have the advantage, arbitrary power cannot be established." *Discourses Concerning Government,* edited by E. G. West (Indianapolis: Liberty Fund, [1698] 1990), 302 (chapter 2, section 30).

3. "Speech on Conciliation with America," March 22, 1775, in ibid., 2:120.

4. "Letter to the Sheriffs of Bristol," 1777, in ibid., 228–229.

5. *Letter* to Mandell Creighton, cited in *Selected Writings of Lord Acton*, 3 volumes, edited by J. Rufus Fears (Indianapolis: Liberty Fund, 1988), volume 3, *Essays in Religion, Politics, and Morality*, 519.

6. "Letter to the Sheriffs of Bristol."

7. Adam Smith, *An Inquiry into the Nature and Causes of the Wealth of Nations*, 2 vols., ed. R. H. Campbell and A. S. Skinner (Volume II of *The Glasgow Edition of the Works and Correspondence of Adam Smith;* Indianapolis: Liberty Fund, 1981), IV.ii.2 (1:456).

8. Adam Smith, *The Theory of Moral Sentiments*, IV.i.10, ed. D. D. Raphael and A. L. Macfie (Volume I of *The Glasgow Edition of the Works and Correspondence of Adam Smith;* Indianapolis: Liberty Fund, 1982), 184–5. An important difference between these two uses of the phrase *invisible hand* is that in *The Wealth of Nations* Smith had the maximization of wealth in mind, while in *The Theory of Moral Sentiments* he had in mind its just distribution. Smith entrusted *both* to the providence of God working through legitimate self-interest. Smith's earliest use of the phrase was in *History of Astronomy*, III.2. There, as one of his modern editors, A. L. Macfie, explains, he attributed only irregular events to supernatural agency; it is apparent, therefore, that his "invisible hand" should not be equated with the deists' "divine Watchmaker." For related discussion, see his *History of Ancient Physics*, 9.

9. St. Augustine, *The City of God*, XIX.xiv; in *A Select Library of the Nicene and Post-Nicene Fathers of the Christian Church*, Series 1, 14 volumes, edited by Philip Schaff (Grand Rapids: Eerdmans, 1978 reprint), 2:410.

10. "The Pretense of Knowledge," F. A. Hayek, *Unemployment and Monetary Policy: Government as Generator of the "Business Cycle,"* ed. Gerald P. O'Driscoll, Jr. (San Francisco: Cato Institute, 1979), 36.

11. C. S. Lewis, *The Abolition of Man* (New York: Macmillan, 1947), 86.

12. St. Augustine, *The City of God,* XIX.xv.

13. Arthur Shenfield, "Capitalism under the Tests of Ethics," *Imprimis* (Hillsdale, MI: Hillsdale College), December 1981; cited in Ronald H. Nash, *Poverty and Wealth: Why Socialism Doesn't Work* (Richardson, TX: Probe Books, 1986), 80.

The Church and Economics

Robert A. Sirico

Robert Sirico is founder and president of the Acton Institute for the Study of Religion and Liberty in Grand Rapids, codirector of the Catholic Information Center, and an adjunct scholar of the Mackinac Center. A former radio and television host at stations in Seattle and Burbank, Father Sirico has served as a parish priest in Minneapolis and as a chaplain to AIDs patients in Bethesda.

His articles on religion, economics, and politics have appeared in numerous publications, including *National Review*, the *Wall Street Journal*, *Commonweal*, the *Catholic World*, *Crisis*, *Reason*, and the *Journal of the American Academy of Religion*. In addition, he has been a contributor to *Freedom with Solidarity* and edited Michael Novak's *Will It Liberate? Questions About Liberation Theology*.

Introduction

Many people are suspicious when they hear religion and economics joined together in a discussion. After all, they reason, the function of religion is to prepare people for the hereafter, while the concern of economics is the allocation of scarce resources in the here-and-now. To mix the two, it has been argued, is to blur the goals of each discipline by making religion mundane and economics sublime.

Put another way, the tension is expressed as follows: Ethics concerns itself with what is right for someone to do, while economics concerns itself with what is rational for someone to do.

I question the presumed contradiction implicit here because I reject the notion that there is an essential contradiction between what philosophers call the "is" and the "ought."

I shall offer this challenge to you by exploring both the nature of economics and its relation to the life of faith.

While I am a Roman Catholic priest, I hope to accomplish this with an ecumenical sensitivity, and a sincere appreciation for the varied faith commitments represented in our Western tradition.

Why the Tension?

Let us start with why, in the popular mind, there is such a tension between the religious way of thinking and the economic way of thinking.

Perhaps the most obvious answer to this question comes from looking at the curriculum offered in most seminaries, whether they be Catholic, Protestant or Jewish. Seminarians rarely, if ever, study economics. The course of studies offered in most seminaries is packed with a wide variety of theological, biblical, homiletic, linguistic, and psychological studies, much of which, depending upon the approach taken, no doubt prove invaluable to those in full-time ministry.

At the same time, you will look far and wide to discover a single course on the basic dynamics of how an economy works. This is not to say that certain economic assumptions are not adopted and presumed within the courses undertaken, which in turn form a backdrop to the way in which these future religious leaders and theologians approach the real world. To see evidence of a seriously flawed understanding of economic liberty we need only look at many of the pronouncements on social and political issues of the mainline churches.

A national survey that was conducted several years ago exemplifies my point. The Roper Center for Public Opinion Research surveyed theology and seminary faculty and found the following:

- 37 percent of the faculty respondents believed the United States "would be better off if it moved toward socialism."

- 37 percent believed that Marxism was consistent with their religious beliefs.

- Nearly 50 percent felt that the redistribution of wealth (as opposed to the production of wealth) was a better way to meet the needs of the poor.

This survey is the most up-to-date poll of religious leaders on economic questions in existence, but I hope that a similar one will be undertaken soon, now that the world has witnessed the colossal failure of the Marxist economic system in Central Europe.

My educated guess is that such a new survey would reveal a shift away from explicit Marxist categories, but I am not confident that, as yet, the underlying premises that caused the respondents to the Roper survey to reply the way they did have altered very much. As long as the same presuppositions are still in place, I fear that similar misunderstandings will continue to arise in various guises, which I shall comment on in due course.

Before I describe what I think some of those guises might be, let me address myself to what I see as some of the basic problems and misconceptions that the religious community will have to confront.

Different Models

There is an intellectual gap between the world of most religious leaders and the world of most of those engaged in finance and economics, that helps to explain some of the hostility between the church and the marketplace. It is as though business people and those who work for the church employ two different models in their day-to-day operations—and indeed they do.

It will help to bridge this gap by looking at these models a little more closely. Simply put, the person who works in the church operates on a "distributionist economic model." By this I mean that on Sunday morning a collection basket is passed. On Monday the bills are paid, acts of charity are attended to, etc. If the Sunday collection comes up short on a regular basis, making it difficult to pay the bills, most preachers begin to turn up the screws a notch or two and lay on another layer of guilt. Thus, many clergy approach the economic world as though it were a pie in need of being divided up. They view the world of money as static, so in order for one to obtain a larger piece of that pie, it is necessary for someone else to get a somewhat smaller piece.

The business person operates from a very different "production model." The entrepreneur talks of *making* money, not collecting it. In other words, for the business person, who must consider the needs, wants, and desires of the consumer, the way to get money is to offer something of value. The economic dimensions of life for these people are dynamic. This process, which we call the free market or free economy, is responsible for the "wealth of nations," a phrase associated in the popular mind with the title of Adam Smith's classic book, but which was first employed in the Book of Isaiah (60:5).

Religion need not, indeed ought not, adopt a bottom line mentality with regard to its mission. There are some matters that simply do not fit within an economic calculus and that cannot be evaluated in terms of "dollars and cents." Some things, in fact some of the most important things in life, cannot be bought and sold in any market. However, before religious leaders choose to pronounce on matters that have specific bearing on the economy, it is only prudent that they become informed.

Another factor that plays into the hostility one frequently encounters regarding the free economy in religious circles comes from a noble, if mistaken, source. Many religious leaders spend a great deal of their lives confronting the wretchedness of poverty in close proximity. Anyone here who has traveled in Third World countries knows the cry of the human heart that yells "Stop!" when confronted with such human misery. Unnecessary poverty angers us, and we want to put an end to it. This sentiment is an exactly proper Christian sentiment.

The problem results when this sentiment is combined with the economic ignorance observed in many religious environments. When this happens the cry against poverty is easily converted into a rage against wealth, which, while understandable, is ill-informed and even deadly. It is deadly because it fails to see that *the amelioration of poverty can only be achieved by the production of wealth.* It is deadly because is seeks to kill the goose that will lay the golden egg; indeed, it will kill the goose that will hatch other golden-egg-laying geese!

The Religious Case for Economic Liberty

I contend that what makes the modern tension between the church and economics so astounding is that economics, specifically free market economics, emerges from religion in the first place. I know this might sound like a surprising claim to some, so allow me to explain.

To understand this, we must first go back to the beginnings of the Jewish, Christian, and Muslim revelation—the Bible, and particularly the first book of the Bible, Genesis.

Nearly everyone knows the dramatic account of God making the heavens and the earth, the ocean, and the dry land, all of the creeping things of the earth, and finally the apex of his creation: Man and Woman. Do you recall God's reaction after each act of creation? Over six times on the first page of Scripture one refrain is repeated over and over again: "God saw that it was good."

This view of the created order, specifically the goodness of the material world that God made, has not been accepted without controversy, even within the Christian tradition. When we look back into the first centuries of Christianity we see that a movement developed which regarded that material world as fundamentally evil, created by a demi-god. This movement was known as Gnosticism, and the Gnostic impulse has surfaced and re-surfaced under many guises throughout Christian history.

The Christian belief in the Incarnation of Jesus Christ is a further embrace of the sacredness of the material world. The Incarnation is the belief that God breaks into human history in the person of Jesus Christ.

Aside from the numerous theological implications to this doctrine, we can discern the beginning of economic reality in both the belief that God created the material world and that God enters this world in the person of Jesus Christ.

To believe that the material world is good is to understand that scarcity is a reality to be dealt with, and this, of course, brings us to the question of economics, which is the study of the allocation of scarce resources.

It is the fundamental goodness of this material dimension of human existence that is at the root of the conflict over the morality of the free market, so in a very real sense, to understand economics one must see the context from which economics emerges in the first place, namely moral theology.

These assertions are not the mere ravings of a priest bent on inserting religion into what has always been and should remain a secular domain. In his expansive survey of the history of economic thought, Joseph Schumpeter writes about the disciples of St. Thomas Aquinas, and makes this astounding concession:

> It is within their system of moral theology and law that economics gained a definite if not separate existence, and it is they who come nearer than does any group to having been the "founders" of scientific economics.[1]

Earlier I noted that the misconceptions of many of those in religious circles arise, from time to time, in altered guises. As I have indicated, I believe this to be partly the result of faulty presuppositions and academic lacunae. It is also the result of an inadequate theology which views matter as essentially evil, and leads to the idea that its possession and use is likewise evil. Throughout the centuries this tendency has recurred in various forms. One sees it in the radical proponents of apostolic poverty like the spiritual Franciscans of the middle ages (not to be confused with the legitimate Franciscans who celebrate God's creation) and in what is left of the Marxist-inspired liberation theologians of today. The implication here is that wealth is axiomatically sinful, and that the wealthy must be relieved of their money in order to be absolved from their sin.

It is useful to look around us to observe some current forms of this error. I suggest two for your consideration:

1. Much of the environmentalist movement encapsulates many of these ideas, especially those parts of it that exhibit a hostility to economic progress and seek to hamper the free economy's ability to coordinate the supply of resources with those in need.

Then, too, there is the religious tone employed by many environmental advocates, a tone which at first glance appears traditionally religious, but in fact overturns the historical Jewish and Christian worldview.

In one of the most widely sold books on these matters, *Earth in the Balance,* Vice President Gore devotes an entire chapter to "Environmentalism of the Spirit," in which he poses this rather sobering question:

> It is time we asked a ... question about ourselves and our relationship to the global environment: When giving us dominion over the earth, did God choose an appropriate technology?

The answer the Vice President offers is of even more concern than the question. He says, " ... the jury is still out."[2]

The jury is out on whom? God? Doesn't the Vice President have things a little backwards? Isn't it God who sits in judgment on us, and not we who sit in judgment on God?

Few, if any, would disagree that the stewardship of our natural environment is a vital responsibility of any civilized society. And that responsibility derives logically from the Judeo-Christian belief that the same God who created our physical universe created man, entrusting him with its care. Thus, our concerns acquire both moral and spiritual overtones.

Yet the vast majority of articles, books, and pronouncements on the subject seem to endow the environment with a sanctity that is curiously denied mankind itself. This is an apparent contradiction of the belief that God created both, and implies that man indeed is the uniquely unnatural inhabitant of his earth. Instead of acknowledging that man's care of the environment is a vital mission, many seem to imply it is his only mission.

In addition to the theological contradictions evident in many of these writings, the economic solutions they prescribe fail to account for the inherent conserving nature of free-market arrangements.

2. The demise of central planning in Central Europe, oddly enough, has not insured a moral victory for the free economy. Many of the former fans of socialism have shifted gears and now lend their support to central planning in another form, notably the welfare state.

Once again, we can certainly understand and even praise the humane sensitivity displayed by those who express deep concern that the need of the poor and most economically marginalized be met. This sensitivity, however, does not exempt them from understanding that a society predicated upon the same or similar economic premises as those in Central Europe will come to the same or similar economic end.

The welfare state fails in its objective for the same reason that socialism failed in its objective.

The key problem with the welfare state is the presupposition that it can observe all social problems and needs and is able to regulate the necessary sectors of society in such a way as to best meet those needs. But no group of planners, no matter how wise and sensitive they might be, can see the deepest needs of the human soul, which frequently are at the root of economic problems. Moreover, when central planning boards become active, they interfere with the free markets' ability to uncover relevant knowledge about local circumstances to meet existing needs. Central planning impedes the market's efficiency and productivity. In other words, the state's pretense to knowledge hinders the necessary order that would emerge naturally, thus preventing the emergence of what would otherwise be more effective and frequently more humane alternatives.

The reluctance of today's religious leaders to approach the desperate problem of poverty in a dynamic manner by tapping into the creativity of the free market is, to a great extent, a new manifestation of the same thinking that has given us many of the errors to which I have alluded.

There is, however, a counter view within the Christian tradition, which is being retrieved in recent days. Historically, the church has always seen the total dynamism of the Christian life as necessarily encompassing the material order, which includes the world of business and finance, by virtue of its belief in the Creation and the Incarnation, as outlined above. It is this approach that I believe will rescue the church from what F.A. Hayek calls the "fatal conceit" of socialism.

The great philosopher Etienne Gilson places the overarching question in exactly the right framework, and does so in a way far more eloquent than I am able. Permit me to quote him at length:

> If one wants to practice science for God's sake, the first condition is to practice it for its own sake, or as if for its own sake, because that is the only way to learn it. . . . It is the same with an art: one must have it before one can put it to God's service. We are told that faith built the medieval cathedrals: no doubt, but faith would not have built anything had there been no architects and craftsmen, If it be true that the west front of Notre Dame is a raising of the soul to God, that does not prevent its being a geometrical composition as well: to build a front that will be an act of charity, one must first understand geometry. We . . . who acclaim the high worth of nature because it is God's work, should show our respect for it by taking as our first rule of action *that piety is never a substitute for technique;* for technique is that without which the most fervent piety is powerless to make use of nature for God's sake. Nothing and nobody obliges a Christian to occupy himself with science, art or philosophy, for there is no lack of other ways of serving God; but *if he has chosen this way of serving him,* the end he puts before himself obliges him to excel; the very intention that guides him compels him to be a good scholar, a good philosopher, a good artist: it is the only way he can become a good servant."

This is the lesson that the church must learn anew, and there is evidence that this is indeed happening.

I wish to employ my own tradition at this point because it is that tradition that I know best.

In 1991, on the one hundredth anniversary of the first modern papal encyclical on Christian social teaching, Pope John Paul II issued what commentators around the world have acknowledged to be a remarkable development in the Catholic Church's perspective on the free market economy.

I cannot offer here a detailed study of this ground-breaking document entitled *Centesimus Annus*. Let me, how-ever, briefly set out some of the highlights of the statement and the ways in which it complements, challenges and deep-ens the philosophy of freedom.

Centesimus Annus identifies socialism as "the cure that would prove worse than the disease," and argues that it stems from a fundamental error that disrespects the human being in his essence as a creature made in the image of God.

In addition, the class struggle is severely condemned, while the role of the state is seen ever more clearly as a regulated one limited to contributing to humanity's striving for increased personal freedom. In this regard, the Pope warns against encroachments into society (which he distin-guishes from the state) and the "business system" which would be to the "detriment of both economic and civil free-dom." Unprecedented in modern Catholic social thought is the expression of pure disenchantment with the welfare state and the fear that such governmental structures "are domi-nated more by bureaucratic ways of thinking than by concern for serving their clients, and which are accompanied by an enormous increase in spending."

There are many other sections of *Centesimus Annus* that would warm the hearts of any proponent of the free market in a virtuous society. What follows are what I believe to be some of the economic and moral ramifications of the encycli-cal:

- that the moral pursuit of private interest, in the divi-sion of labor and what is called the vocation of entrepreneur-ship, need not serve individual good at the expense of the commonweal;

- that a stable currency ensures the stability of the entire monetary system, protects savings, promotes investment, and permits the price system to function properly in all sectors of the economy;

- that the free market economy is fueled by a process of discovery that carefully balances the scarcity of the world's resources with the unlimited demands of consumers, and that market liberalism is superior to alternatives in performing this task;

- that "by intervening and depriving society of its responsibility," individuals in the state sector (politicians and bureaucrats) tend to serve their own interests rather than those of society at large, and that their expressed interests tend to destroy the social cooperation that would allow private citizens to "act as neighbors to those in need";

- that the government ought not to be the resource of first resort for those who find themselves in economic need;

- that the size and influence of any government should be limited so as to provide greater freedom to the individual in accordance with the thrust of his or her nature as a member of the human community and as a child of God.

The turn that *Centesimus Annus* represents on the part of the world's largest Christian religion toward authentic human liberty as a principle for social organization indicates that a new dialogue has begun between the world of the church and the world of economics.

Conclusion

It is to be expected that in the newly emerging dialogue between economic liberals and the church new tensions will arise requiring each side of the dialogue to deepen its understanding of itself and its domain of expertise.

One of the sources of tension will no doubt be that economists often refuse to speak in normative terms, and they often act as if they should not. Likewise, those charged with pronouncing on morality in public and economic life do not yet have strong sympathies with the ethic of capitalism, if they are sympathetic with it at all.

Most people are content to settle for a system that seems to reconcile the "ethics" of socialism with the "productivity" of capitalism. Yet ethics and productivity should be and must be reconciled. If we continue to promote an "ethics" of socialism, it will eventually endanger the institutions that support the productive capacity of capitalism. It is not a trivial fact that every step away from the free market is a step away from voluntarism and every step toward interventionism is a step away from liberty. It speaks to the essence of what it means to act virtuously.

It is sometimes said that no one dreams of capitalism. This must change. Rightly understood, capitalism is simply the name for the economic component of the natural order of liberty. It means expansive ownership of property, fair and equal rules for all, economic security through prosperity, strict adherence to the boundaries of ownership, opportunity for charity, wise resource use, creativity, growth, development, prosperity, abundance, and most of all, economic application of the principle that every human person has dignity and should have that dignity respected.

It is a dream worthy of our spiritual imagination.

In *Tractatus Theologico-Politicus*, Spinoza also articulates a principle worthy of our consideration:

> Simplicity and truth of character are not produced by the constraint of laws, nor by the authority of the state, and absolutely no one can be forced or legislated into a state of blessedness; the means required are faithful and brotherly love, sound education, and, above all, free use of individual judgment.

Notes

1. Joseph Schumpeter, *History of Economic Analysis* (New York: Oxford University Press, 1954), 97.

2. Al Gore, *Earth in the Balance: Ecology and the Human Spirit*, 238.

The Hidden History of Capitalism

Burton W. Folsom, Jr.

Burton W. Folsom, Jr. is a professor of history at Murray State University in Kentucky where he has taught United States history since 1976. His articles have appeared in sources such as the *Wall Street Journal*, the *Pacific Historical Review*, the *Journal of Southern History*, the *Journal of American Studies*, the *World and I*, the *Freeman, and Human Events*. He also is the editor of the journal *Continuity* and author of *The Progressive Era in Nebraska, 1900–1920* (AMS Press, 1993), *Entrepreneurs vs. the State: A New Look at the Rise of Big Business in America, 1840–1920* (Young America's Foundation, 1987, reissued in 1991 as *The Myth of the Robber Barons*), and *Urban Capitalists: Entrepreneurs and City Growth in Pennsylvania's Lackawanna and Lehigh Regions, 1800–1920* (Johns Hopkins University Press, 1981).

In the ongoing war of ideas in American history, those who advocate government action as an engine of economic development have been encouraged by a general and all-too-human tendency to avoid thinking deeply. Because we have a long history of government intervention in the economy, the assumption—both among those who design government programs and among the constituencies that support them—has usually been that government action accomplishes its objectives. Even people who have reservations about bureaucratic inefficiency reason that we wouldn't have turned to government so many times in the past if government hadn't accomplished *something.*

Three Assumptions about Capitalism

This shallow conclusion dovetails with another set of assumptions: First, that the free market, with its economic un-

49

certainty, competitive stress, and constant potential for failure, needs the steadying hand of government regulation; second, that businessmen tend to be unscrupulous, reflecting the classic cliché image of the "robber baron," eager to seize any opportunity to steal from the public; and third, that because government can mobilize a wide array of forces across the political and business landscape, government programs therefore can move the economy more effectively than can the varied and often conflicting efforts of private enterprise.

But the closer we look at public-sector economic initiatives, the more difficult it becomes to defend government as a wellspring of progress. Indeed, an honest examination of our economic history—going back long before the 20th century—reveals that, more often than not, when government programs and individual enterprise have gone head-to-head, the private sector has achieved more progress at less cost with greater benefit to consumers and the economy at large.

Competition vs. Subsidy in the Steamship Industry

America's early experience with the steamship industry provides an illustrative case. By the 1840s, the technology of steam-powered water transport had reached the point where it became practical to build large, ocean-going vessels, and steamships began plying the route between New York City and Liverpool, England. An enterprising fellow named Edward K. Collins approached the U.S. Congress with a plan to develop a steamship fleet that could compete with Britain's Cunard Company. Since the Cunard operation was subsidized by the British government, Collins asked Congress to provide him with a grant of $3 million to underwrite construction of five vessels and a yearly supplement of $385,000 so he could run his line at the competitive fare of $200 per passenger and undercut Cunard's rates for carrying freight and mail.

Collins was what may be called a "political entrepreneur." Playing skillfully on congressional fears about British domination of the transatlantic trade, and promising that his ships could serve as the basis of a merchant marine fleet in the event of war, Collins got his money. He then proceeded to build four very large and luxurious ships, instead of the five smaller vessels provided for in the agreement, and he took far longer than anticipated to get his fleet into operation.

Collins ran his ships on the same schedule as Cunard, sailing every two weeks, and he often did beat Cunard's crossing time by one day, though at considerably higher operating costs. But while he had promised Congress that his yearly subsidy could eventually be phased out, he was soon lobbying for annual increases to about $500,000, $600,000, $700,000, and then to more than $800,000 per year.

Cornelius Vanderbilt, who had made his mark as an operator of river steamboats, approached Congress with a proposal for an "Atlantic ferry," offering to match Collins' two-week sailing schedule at half the cost of Collins' subsidy. Congress debated Vanderbilt's proposal. But having made a commitment to Collins—and by now a considerable investment as well—Congress turned Vanderbilt down.

Vanderbilt was undeterred. He went into operation without a subsidy, using privately financed ships, set up a self-insurance arrangement by which he was able to save on payments to outside insurers, and ran his ships at slower speeds to save fuel. He also reduced the fare, and he invented a new, cheaper passenger class, by which people could travel below decks, in what was called *steerage,* for as little as $30. Vanderbilt's "sardine class" made it possible for many immigrants to come to America.

After a year, Vanderbilt's operation was flourishing, and Collins, in serious trouble from competition with Vanderbilt, went to Congress to ask that his subsidy be raised, yet again, to almost $900,000. Collins wined and dined key members aboard his luxurious ships and was able to convince the congressmen to conclude that *since they started with Collins, it would be dishonest to take his money away now.*

But Collins recognized that each time he went back to Congress for more money, the vote was closer. He decided that if he couldn't beat Vanderbilt on price, he would concentrate on beating his crossing time, demonstrating that the Collins line clearly offered the most efficient way to get from Liverpool to New York City. This strategy had its dangers. Long beset with maintenance problems because their engines were too large for their hulls, Collins' ships began to feel the strain of this high-speed policy. Two of the ships—half his fleet—sunk, killing almost 500 passengers, and Collins faced the humiliation of going back to Congress to beg for more money for construction of a replacement vessel and an increase in his subsidy.

Again Congress funded him. But at $1 million to build, the new ship was so poorly constructed that it had to be sold at auction after its first voyage—at a $900,000 loss. When Collins went back to Congress for still *more* money to build yet *another* ship, he was finally turned down.

It is interesting to look at the reaction in Congress after being embarrassed again and again by the subsidies to Collins. Senator Judah Benjamin of Louisiana said, "I believe [the Collins line] has been most miserably managed." Senator Robert Hunter of Virginia went further. "The whole system was wrong," he said. "It ought to have been left, like any other trade, to competition." Senator John Thompson of Kentucky insisted, "Give neither this line nor any other a subsidy. Let the Collins line die. I want a *tabula rasa* . . . a new beginning."

Collins had his subsidy stripped and had to compete head to head—unsupported—with Vanderbilt. Within a year, Collins went bankrupt, and Vanderbilt was the dominant force on the seas from the American side.

Competition vs. Subsidy in the Railroad Industry

It would be comforting to report that the U.S. learned its lesson about federal subsidies from the Collins/Vanderbilt experience. Unfortunately, less than a decade later, would-be railroad builders were coming to Congress begging for money to span the nation with transcontinental lines. Congress subsidized three transcontinental railroads: the Union Pacific, the Central Pacific, and later the Northern Pacific.

These companies, which were provided with money and land by the government, had no incentive to build their lines efficiently, along straight routes with even grades and proper materials. Eventually they went bankrupt. The Union Pacific and the Central Pacific did so only after eating up forty-four million acres of free land and $61 million in cash loans. Large sections of the lines they did complete soon had to be rebuilt and sometimes even relocated due to shoddy construction.

The privately funded Great Northern, which, by contrast, operated on a shoestring budget, was a success. Unlike his competitors, James J. Hill built the Great Northern for durability and efficiency. "What we want," he said, "is the best possible line, shortest distance, lowest grades, and least curvature that we can build." That meant he personally supervised the surveying and construction. "I find that it pays to be where the money is being spent," he noted. He believed that building a functional and durable product actually saved money. For example, he usually imported high quality Bessemer rails, even though they cost more than those made in America. He was thinking about the future, and quality building cut costs in the long run. When Hill constructed the solid granite Stone Arch bridge—2,100 feet long, 28 feet wide, and 82 feet high across the Mississippi River—it became *the* Minneapolis landmark for decades. Yet today Hill is regarded as just another member among the ranks of greedy, amoral "get rich-quick" capitalists.

Competition vs. Subsidy in the Steel Industry

Even when entrepreneurs have led the way entirely, developing industries in fields where federal money had never been involved, suspicion and resentment about the motives and methods of the "robber barons" have encouraged government to thrust itself into business—often with absurd results, as the example of Andrew Carnegie and the steel industry shows.

When Carnegie founded Carnegie Steel in 1872, the biggest steel producer in the world was England and the going price of steel rails was about $60 per ton. Carnegie was an eager innovator. He adopted the revolutionary Bessemer process and introduced new accounting methods to make his operations more efficient, applied a merit pay system to reward his workers, and implemented many employee-suggested ideas. Carnegie Steel became *so* efficient that by 1900 the company could produce steel rails at $11 per ton, and its rail output surpassed that of all the steel mills in England combined. Other U.S. firms followed Carnegie's lead, and America became the dominant steel producer of the world.

But the success of American steel companies and the great wealth of their owners was not regarded as a testament to the power of free enterprise. Instead it became a cause for concern. The common attitude was summed up by Senator Ben Tillman of South Carolina, who referred to the steelmakers as "greedy and hoggish." Where there was profit, there had to be price gouging. President Woodrow Wilson became convinced that Congress should establish a government-operated steel mill to compete with the private manufacturers, and after much debate, a federal steel facility was built in Charleston, West Virginia, at a cost of $17.5 million.

It was a blessing to Wilson that he became too ill to concern himself with the results of his venture, which set about the task of producing steel armor plate. Indeed, armor plate *was* produced—at roughly *$800 per ton!* When the Republicans won the next election and Harding succeeded Wilson in the White House, the Charleston plant was quietly closed.

Time and again, experience has shown that while private enterprise, carried on in an environment of open competition, delivers the best products and services at the best price, government intervention stifles initiative, subsidizes inefficiency, and raises costs. But if we have difficulty learning from history, it is often because our true economic history is largely hidden from us. We would be hard pressed to find anything about Vanderbilt's success or Collins' government-backed failure in the steamship business by examining the conventional history textbooks or taking a history course at most colleges or universities. Likewise, we probably wouldn't learn how the three subsidized railroads went bankrupt while the unsubsidized line succeeded, or about the federal government's disastrous foray into the steelmaking business. The information simply isn't included. I should know: I received a Ph.D. in U.S. economic history, and I never encountered these stories until after I was out of graduate school.

Rewriting History: A Lesson in Anticapitalism

But missing information isn't the only problem. In some cases, the facts of American history have been so thoroughly distorted as to make economic understanding impossible. The historical treatment of one early experience with adjusting income tax rates provides a good example. Irwin Unger, in his text, *These United States*, describes the tax policy of U.S. Treasury Secretary Andrew Mellon, who served under three presidents, but mainly President Calvin Coolidge, between 1921 and 1932:

> [Harding and Coolidge] allowed Secretary of the Treasury Andrew Mellon, a Pittsburgh industrialist and one of the world's richest men, to pursue "soak-the-poor" policies.... He persuaded Congress to reduce income tax rates at the upper level, while leaving those at the bottom untouched. Between 1920 and 1929, Mellon won further victories for his drive to shift the tax burden onto the backs of the middle and wage-earning classes.

Similarly, in their textbook, *The National Experience*, Arthur Schlesinger, Jr., and John Blum note:

> It was better [Mellon] argued, to place the burden of taxes on the lower-income groups, for taxing the rich inhibited their investments and thus retarded economic growth. A share of the tax-free profits of the rich, Mellon reassured the country, would ultimately trickle down to the middle- and lower-income groups in the form of salaries and wages.

This is the picture we get from two of the leading American history textbooks. But what are the actual facts of Mellon's and Coolidge's tax policy? In the 1920s, the tax rate on the highest income group went from 73 percent down to 24 percent—a three-fold reduction. At the same time, the tax rate on the lowest income group went down from four percent to one half of one percent—an *eight-fold* reduction. And in 1929, after Mellon and Coolidge had implemented their tax cutting policy, the government was collecting some 30 percent more tax revenues than had been collected with the higher tax rates of the early 1920s—an experience which would be repeated years later in the tax reductions of the Kennedy and Reagan administrations.

We can speculate on ideological motives that may have prompted these historians to present the kind of picture they did, but the bottom line for us as citizens is that we cannot draw appropriate conclusions about the proper role of government from missing or distorted information. Only when the true facts are available can real debate begin.

Capitalism as the Most Moral System of Economic Exchange

Even armed with the evidence, however, what we need to realize is that competition is not painless, and progress is not easy. There are losers as well as winners in our history, and we need to understand them both without blaming either group. This means, of course, that we have to learn what capitalism is all about. In the words of philosopher Ronald Nash, "Capitalism is quite simply the most moral system and the most equitable system of economic exchange." Why does he make this assertion? Because throughout our history, capitalism has provided the opportunity to compete—the chance for individuals with ambition to get into the game, to test their talents and abilities and ideas against those of everyone else, unrestrained by the Old World strictures of landed wealth and rigid social class. When those individuals have been able to pursue their dreams, free from the distorting influence of government interference, progress has been made and society in general has benefited enormously.

Ethics and the Marketplace

Thomas M. Nies

Thomas Nies' experience in the computer field began in 1962 when he joined the IBM Corporation. He remained there for six years in a variety of technical and marketing positions and became project director for one of the first on-line installations.

Recognizing the need for quality software to complement hardware systems, in 1968 he founded Cincom Systems, Inc., which he continues to serve as president and chief executive officer. Today, Cincom is one of the world's largest and best established software companies with over sixty marketing and support locations around the globe. Nearly two-thirds of its interests are international. It is a primary supplier of data management systems, high level application development languages, manufacturing applications, text processing, and project management software.

The Marketplace

A marketplace is a free area (usually but not necessarily geographic) where goods and services may be exchanged. It is based on a wide variety of laws and absolutes like weight, hours in the day, and miles traveled as well as on subjective values like quality, desirability, and utility.

Aside from the entrepreneurs and managers who actually run a business, there are three basic types of individuals who help carry on free exchange in the marketplace. First of all, there is the investment capitalist. He is the one with wealth who wants his wealth to work for him and make him richer. His primary vision of the purpose of a business is to maximize investor value. He does not buy shares in the stock market in order to try to further the cause of General Motors and IBM, or to provide more automobiles and computers, or to boost the GNP. He is trying to increase freely his own personal wealth by buying stocks that will go up in value and by selling them before they go down.

The second basic type is the worker. The worker's vision of the purpose of a business is to provide highly compensated employment without exploitation. But wise workers realize that, if their best interests are to prevail, a business has to survive. One of the great labor leaders of the nineteenth century, Samuel Gompers, said that the first responsibility of the business, therefore, is not to its employees but to earn a profit. However, in this process the worker must always be free to work in whatever field or career he chooses.

The third basic type is the customer. Speaking for the customer, Peter Drucker, who is widely regarded as one of the greatest writers on management principles in the twentieth century, says that a business should provide goods and services that the customer needs and desires. But he, too, understands the necessity of profit, so he adds that the purpose of a business is not just to create and serve customers, maximize shareholder value, or provide employment, but to earn the minimum profit necessary for its own long-term survival. Again, freedom must be a key characteristic of this system. Customers must be free to buy according to their own choice.

Ethics

In the marketplace, ethics have a vital role. Ethics constitute the science of how we *ought* to behave. I emphasize the word "ought" for an important reason. It implies—indeed, it demands—that we be free. Only if we are free do we have choices between how we *ought* to behave and how we *do* behave.

Ethics, in turn, demand justice. And justice demands fair laws. Fair laws must transcend the opinion of individuals; they cannot merely reflect current popular opinion or majority rule. How do we know this to be true? We have only to recall that slavery was once legal in the United States and that the Supreme Court ruled in its infamous *Dred Scott* decision that slaves had no more rights than cattle.

In other words, fair laws must transcend society itself, and they must be absolute. But, in recent years, many of us have sought the opposite: a society that transcends laws and laws that change according to the mood of the times. We Americans want more liberty, it seems, and not more justice. Once again, history could teach us an important lesson: The bloody tragedy of the French Revolution proved once and for all that liberty without law descends into license. Anything goes in such a society; no one of us can be held guilty for our beliefs or actions and no one of us has any real ties that binds us to others.

No Man Is an Island

Ever since the twentieth century novelist Ernest Hemingway discovered the seventeenth century poet and clergyman John Donne and his maxim that "no man is an island," our modern culture has rightly emphasized the ties that *do* bind us. All members of society are interdependent. But, in the larger sense, all of God's creation is not only interdependent, but "interpenetrating." The plant consumes minerals. It then transforms those nonliving substances into a part of itself, a living thing, and that living thing is thus able to create more living things. A single, tiny acorn produces not only an oak tree but, in time, a vast forest of oak trees. The animal that consumes plants transforms them into a part of itself, a feeling, sensory animal with the capacity to produce whole herds of other animals.

Human beings consume, transform, and create in exactly the same way. In a very real way, then, each of us is formed by others, and we help to form them. Our social, economic, political, and religious lives are also interpenetrating, despite our frequent, mistaken attempts at compartmentalization. Thus, there is no one of us that can be understood as merely *homo economicus*.

And that means that our ethics matter, and our character counts. Indeed, character is the key issue if not the only issue; character is the sum and substance of all we are. Each one of us is a moral person created to live and function within a social order. And a moral person knows that he ought to behave in a certain way which he knows is ethical. And ethics must be defined by a power which he knows transcends the individual person.

Morality, Freedom, and Economic Systems

That power, of course, is God.

How do we learn about God? We usually learn about Him within the bounds of the oldest human institution—the family. It is families, not discrete individuals, that tend to organize themselves as communities, states, and nations. And these entities institute laws for the protection of individual and family rights. At the same time, families, communities, states, and nations help to propagate a good and responsible civil order that becomes the basis for justice, fair laws, and sound governance.

Learning about God and determining our ethics based on His will is rooted in the religious values and beliefs that sustain all of the rest of our civil order. If our nation is to succeed, it must be true to its religious foundations. This principle is applicable to the marketplace. As the introduction to this volume states, religion and morality are "the basic foundation of economics. Although every system has intellectual theories, abstract principles, models, graphs, and formulas, it also has underlying values." And the introduction concludes: "On every issue society faces, from the environment to homelessness, from inflation to taxes, the dividing line is between those who regard individual freedom as the best solution and those who advocate more government. And in each case it comes down to a matter of profoundly different values and views about the morality of the marketplace."

How do the economic systems of the twentieth century rate in terms of morality? How do they value freedom? There is an old set of humorous definitions that perhaps answers this question best:

Communism. Communism has failed where ever it has been practiced, but it has remained dominant as an ideal for most of the twentieth century. Imagine you have two cows. The communist government takes both of these cows from you yet forces you to take care of them, and it only gives you enough milk back to enable you to survive.

Socialism. Socialism is another failed economic system, but it still manages to hang on in many countries. Again, imagine you have two cows. The socialist government takes one and gives the other to your neighbor. Then it taxes you for the cost of caring for your neighbor's new cow.

Fascism. Fascism has also failed in this century. Many people mistakenly call it a right-wing system, but in reality it is closer to communism and socialism because it presupposes that the individual exists to serve the state. If you have two cows, the fascist government takes both cows and then sells you the milk.

National socialism. This is a variant of socialism and fascism that was tried by the Nazi government in Germany. If you have two cows, the national socialist government takes away both cows but forbids you to complain.

Capitalism. This is the economic system that has done so much to bring prosperity to the world, especially to America. It is the only system that is based on the idea that the state exists to serve the individual. If you have two cows under capitalism, you are free to sell one of them and buy a bull. In time, you will have many cows and more milk than you will ever need. But today capitalism is threatened by the growth of bureaucracy. Bureaucrats in a capitalist system are just like bureaucrats in all other systems; they take both cows, shoot one, milk the other, and then pour the rest of the milk down the drain.

The Judeo-Christian Tradition

Humor aside, we ought to remember that capitalism is superior to all other economic systems because it is based in some important ways on the Christian tradition. I do not wish to argue which form of Christianity (or any other form of religion) is best, but I do wish to note that there are significant differences in the way each believes economics should be conducted. Some Christian religions emphasize certain aspects while others do not. The goal here is simply to try to discuss how these aspects inform people's ethics and determine what impact religion has on the marketplace.

The Protestant view, while it respects the large body of thought developed by church leaders, past and present, is not built on a hierarchy of authority. It holds that private, individual interpretation of the Bible is possible. Each person decides for himself what the Bible means and, except in the most general way (which holds that the meaning of some of the language of the Bible is plain and obvious to everyone and that pastors can be helpful in guiding a person in his search for meaning), there is no higher authority to dictate to him. It is this view that inspired two of the world's strongest defenders of the morality of the marketplace: the eighteenth century Scottish moral philosopher, Adam Smith, who invented the theory of the "invisible hand" in the economy, and the twentieth century American president, Ronald Reagan, who updated the theory and called it "enlightened self-interest."

This view has also been responsible for what we have come to know as the "Protestant work ethic." Many observers hold that it was this spirit, more than any other, that built America. The notion has been that God blesses the hardworking and that their success is a sign of His favor. But although economic success is a sign of God's favor, this does not mean success at any price. Might does not make right. The ends do not justify the means. And the marketplace is not the testing ground for the survival of the fittest.

The Catholic view is that personal ethics and conduct in the marketplace, like all things in life, must be based on Church doctrine that has either been handed down through the centuries or produced by recognized intellectual leaders within the Church who are charged with interpreting the traditional tenets and principles of Catholicism. This view recognizes the possession of private property as a God-given right. Possessing property is a part of our nature. We must have the right to property in order to be free.

In this context, it is important to remember that our founding fathers debated for a long time before they settled on the words "life, liberty, and the pursuit of happiness" in the Declaration of Independence. They also considered using the words "life, liberty, and the right to property," but chose the former as it seemed more all-encompassing. They did firmly believe that property is a natural right and that it is not only a right that we need in order to be free but that we need in order to faithfully and rightly promulgate our duties and responsibilities as citizens.

The traditional Catholic view also emphasizes the concept of Christian stewardship. Our responsibilities and duties to fellow human beings are vital in all economic matters. Excessive wealth and greed of all types is condemned. St. Thomas Aquinas, the thirteenth century theologian who was responsible for articulating much of the Church's doctrine, states explicitly that the one truly in need has a greater right to property held in excess than does the original property holder. And he (the original property holder) may not withhold what is required by the needy. He is morally duty-bound to share his excess. But the Catholic view forbids anyone, including the government, from taking property by force (and this includes legal force) simply in order to redistribute it.

In America today, the traditional Protestant and Catholic views have come under attack. The slogan, "Tax the rich" has become the new battle cry for those do not understand or respect the ethics of the marketplace. They want not only to confiscate much of the current earnings of the rich, but much of the property that the next generation is due to inherit. They want, in words, not just to penalize the rich (and their definition of this term is loose indeed) but to take away one of our natural, God-given rights. What we work for, what we own, what we sacrifice to achieve, what we want to pass on to our children—all of these things are to be subjugated to the whims of the state.

America as a Good Nation

Bishop Fulton Sheen taught that we struggle on three levels. The first level is the material or territorial level. The second is the human or interpersonal level. And the third is the divine level. He noted that as we move upward from the material to the human and to the divine level, our actions and our motives become more pure, more noble, more uplifting, and more long-serving. And so, it is altogether fitting and proper that this volume is devoted to the theme of morality and the marketplace. We must always be mindful that at all times we should function on all three of these levels so, at the end of the day, and at the end of our lives, we can measure how well we have lived up to our ethics.

In no other way can the marketplace be ethical, in no other way can we, or America, be good. One of the most important observations ever made about America was that it was a good nation long before it became a great one. We should remember this, and we should also remember that once a nation ceases to be good, it ceases to be great. No matter how powerful it may have been, once it ceases to be a good or moral nation, it will inevitably fall into the dustbin of history.

God and the Economy: Is Capitalism Moral?

Doug Bandow

Doug Bandow is a senior fellow at the Cato Institute and a nationally syndicated columnist with the Copley News Service. He has served as a special assistant to President Reagan and as editor of *Inquiry* Magazine and has written for numerous publications, including *Harper's*, the *New Republic*, the *Washington Post*, the *New York Times*, and the *Wall Street Journal*.

His books include *The Politics of Plunder: Misgovernment in Washington* (Transaction, second printing, 1990), *Human Resources and Defense Manpower* (Heritage Foundation, 1989), *Beyond Good Intentions: A Biblical View of Politics* (Good News Publishers, 1988), and *Unquestioned Allegiance* (Heritage Foundation, 1986), and he has edited *U.S. Aid to the Developing World: A Free Market Agenda* (Heritage Foundation, 1985) and *Protecting the Environment: A Free Market Strategy* (Heritage Foundation, 1986).

Collectivism is in retreat around the globe, yet it continues to retain some support in the American religious community. If recent events demonstrate conclusively that Marxism does not work in practice, many religious idealists persist in believing that capitalism is immoral in theory. The criticism has long been ecumenical: Catholic liberation theologians dressed Marxist class analysis in religious clothing while left-wing evangelicals equated markets and materialism.

Free Exchange

Some observers have seen virtually every human ill arising from capitalism, a system ultimately based on the simple

---

This chapter originally appeared in *Terra Nova*, Vol. 1, No. 4 (Summer, 1992). Reprinted by permission of the author.

principle of free exchange. For instance, Danny Collum, an editor of *Sojourners* magazine, complained a decade ago that:

> ... the gross inequalities of wealth and poverty in the United States are the natural result of a social, political, and economic system that places the maximization of private profit above all other social goals. The human, social, cultural, and spiritual benefits that would result from a more just distribution of wealth and power will never show up on the all-important quarterly profit and loss statement.

Britain's Andrew Kirk wouldn't even accept the claim that capitalism promotes liberty. A market economy, he wrote, "certainly increases the freedom of some, but always and inevitably at the expense of the freedom of others."

At heart, Christianity poses a radical challenge to the appropriateness of every human action and institution. "Do not love the world or anything in the world," wrote the Apostle John in his first epistle. "If anyone loves the world the love of the Father is not in him. For everything in the world—the cravings of sinful man, the lust of his eyes and the boasting of what he has and does—comes not from the Father but from the world. The world and its desires pass away, but the man who does the will of God lives forever" (I John 2:15–17).

The Spirit of Christian Love

Capitalism is therefore not exempt from scrutiny. It is an imperfect institution, administered by sinful men, just like any other. But the harshest critics suggest that a market economy is not just defective, but is fundamentally inconsistent with the Christian faith. For example, in the view of John Cort, author of *Christian Socialism*, "a Christian could, not to mention should, be a socialist." Further, he writes:

> the "spirit of Christian love" cannot be reduced to a political imperative, granted, but it most certainly has a political dimension. Feeding the hungry and clothing the naked are not precisely identical with a systematic redistribution of wealth, but in the present situation, of gross inequality, obscene

wealth and wretched poverty, they most certainly cry to heaven for both systematic and unsystematic redistribution.

Is he right? Is capitalism fundamentally immoral?

Despite Cort's emotional appeal to the "spirit of Christian love," the Bible does not specifically speak to the proper degree of government intervention in the economy. There is no explicit endorsement of any type of economic system, no equation of capitalism or socialism with the Kingdom of God. Old Testament Israel placed some restrictions on debts, interest, and property transfers but allowed relatively free economic exchange. The so-called "jubilee laws" were tied to the Israelites' special status as God's people—secular America is therefore not a good analogue to religious Israel—and did not transfer property ownership from people to the state. The Gospels and epistles of the New Testament are remarkably free of any economic policy recommendations. Indeed, writes Paul Heyne, a professor at the University of Washington, "What we do find in the New Testament is an extraordinary disregard for almost everything in which economists are interested." In the absence of a holy ideology, one must answer a more subtle question: Which system is more consistent with Biblical principles?

The Bible on the Role of the State

In discussing capitalism it is important to distinguish a competitive market economy from systems that merely involve some private property ownership. Kleptocracies and crony capitalist regimes exist around the globe; particularly obscene are many Latin American governments, where an elite has long used political power to exploit the rest of the population. Such systems are far closer to socialism than to capitalism, however, since they involve pervasive government economic control.

Christ's message is clear: Believers are not to place their faith in Mammon or any of the other idols of this world. But while the Bible is long on injunctions involving man's relation to God and his neighbors, it says far less about the role of the state. The fact that people are not to trust in material goods does not mean that economic decision-making should be placed in the hands of a coercive institution such as government.

The early Christians, at least in Jerusalem, shared their material goods with the needy in the community of faith. However, these voluntary followers of Christ never attempted to forcibly redistribute the assets of non-Christians or even fellow believers. Indeed, the Apostles consistently taught that giving was not mandatory as it was under the law of the old covenant. Peter stated that members of the Jerusalem church had no obligation to sell their property and turn over their proceeds to the body; Paul refused to order the members of the Corinthian church to provide assistance for the believers in Jerusalem. Of course, both men expressed the hope that their readers would behave generously. Wrote Paul: "Each man should give what he has decided in his heart to give, not reluctantly or under compulsion, for God loves a cheerful giver" (II Corinthians 9:7).

A faith that refuses to order its adherents to give not surprisingly provides little support for using the state to make others give. And the commandment against theft should raise at least some questions as to when collective action exceeds Biblical authority. Moreover, there are other scriptural reasons to be more skeptical than supportive of proposals to concentrate economic power in the government's hands.

Most importantly, the Christian faith recognizes that all human institutions are flawed, and that sinful men are likely to misuse their power. Consider the Apostle John's vision in Revelation of a hideous "Beast" state with expansive power, including over people's economic affairs (no one could buy or sell anything without the Beast's mark).

Less apocalyptic but nevertheless equally striking is the prophet Samuel's warning when the Israelites ask God for a king:

> He will take your sons and make them serve with his chariots and horses, and they will run in front of his chariots. Some

he will assign to be commanders of thousands and commanders of fifties, and others to plow his ground and reap his
harvest, and still others to make weapons of war and equip-
ment for his chariots. He will take your daughters to be per-
fumers and cooks and bakers. He will take the best of your
fields and vineyards and olive groves and give them to his
attendants. He will take a tenth of your grain and of your
vintage and give it to his officials and attendants. Your men-
servants and maidservants and the best of your cattle and
donkeys he will take for his own use. He will take a tenth of
your flocks, and you yourselves will become his slaves. When
that day comes, you will cry out for relief from the king you
have chosen, and the Lord will not answer you in that day (I
Samuel 8:11–18).

Economic Liberty: The Prerequisite for Other Freedoms

Most religious critics of capitalism respond that they op-
pose Stalinist communism and instead advocate some variant
of democratic collectivism. But economic liberty is a prerequisite for other freedoms. Countries such as South Korea
and Taiwan have used market economies to prosper, demands for political reform have then naturally grown. Capitalist reforms in China have helped create a more prosperous
population, which has grown increasingly restive under traditional communist political controls.

Economic freedom is important because it helps dis-
perse power, allowing the development of private institutions—associations, corporations, think tanks, labor unions,
and universities, for instance—that can counterbalance state
power. Moreover, private property is necessary for the exercise of many political rights. If you can't buy a printing press
or TV station, hire a hall, or sell newspapers, you have no
freedom of the press. The Soviet Union's great conundrum
in the early 1980s was the personal computer, necessary for
economic progress but a potentially devastating weapon in
the hands of dissidents.

Nevertheless, there is a spiritual sterility to market capitalism that bothers many religious people. While a number
of former East Germans, for instance, deplore their old po-

lice state, they still dislike the gaudy, individualistic materialism of the West. Andrew Kirk contends that capitalism assumes "that the main purpose of man's life is the pursuit of happiness to be achieved by the constant expansion of goods and services" and that this is thereby "the basis of our daily political and economic life."

However, all men are fallen and sinful; greed and envy are common to man, not products of particular social systems. Capitalism allows those who have dedicated themselves to the pursuit of Mammon to live that way, but it also lets believers like Kirk decide to fulfill their lives differently. Kirk, for one, became affiliated with a religious institute, a choice he could not have made in the socialist East. Capitalist America has similarly proved receptive to communal religious sects like the Hutterites.

The hallmark of a relatively unregulated market economy is freedom of choice, and some people will undoubtedly use their liberty to go grievously wrong. But Marxism is profoundly materialistic, and political life in such societies revolves around gaining access to a relatively small pool of consumer goods—thus the avariciousness of the *nomenklatura*, the ruling elite, and the ubiquitous queues in the one-time communist world. The average citizen of a socialist state does not care any less about possessing shoes, washing machines, VCRs, and cars than an American; he is simply less able to satisfy his desires.

Competition and Cooperation

A related argument is that capitalism relies on destructive competition rather than constructive cooperation. Competition is obviously important to a market economy, but it has proved to be an extraordinarily valuable social tool. Private monopolies usually break down quickly because of competition, unless they have government support. Competition drives down the price of consumer goods, enabling people of even modest incomes to acquire clothing, food, and shelter. Competition also drives innovators to seek to design better products for less.

Indeed, while competition is a hallmark of capitalism, so too is cooperation. For only by cooperating—with customers, suppliers, and workers—can a businessman succeed. In a system of state control firms can force their products on reluctant buyers, extract supplies from reluctant producers, and mandate work from reluctant employees. A private firm, however, can only succeed by inducing the cooperation of all of these parties. While money may seem a crass inducement, it is also effective; moreover, many firms where people group together voluntarily, in contrast to collectivist systems, generate *esprit de corps* that reflects a variety of nonmaterial values.

Understanding Poverty Amid Plenty

Perhaps the most fundamental criticism of capitalism is the prevalence of poverty amid plenty. The desperation of the inner city was given added publicity after the riots in Los Angeles and some supporters of Cuba's Castro have responded to criticism of his repressive tactics by arguing that there are no homeless people in Havana. Indeed, Andrew Kirk wrote, before the collapse of the East in 1989, that "Marxism has exalted collective freedom—the freedom of everyone to enjoy a basically dignified life." Yet it is now painfully obvious that poverty was pervasive and income differentials were hideous in those nations. Acquisitive ruling elites may have cloaked their greed in humanitarian socialist rhetoric, but the reality of their systems was quite different.

Truly free market societies, in contrast to statist systems such as Brazil, have also performed well in enhancing the economic status of all their citizens. Taiwan, for instance, has enjoyed a dramatic increase in literacy, life expectancy, and equality of income distribution as it has expanded economically. Even in the United States those who are poor live far better than the bulk of the populations of many Third World states. In short, without production there is nothing to redistribute. Only in a capitalist economy may one meaningfully advocate extensive government transfer programs.

Yet today the state does far more to harm than help the poor. Indeed, much of the poverty in the United States is the result of government policy, often at the behest of powerful special interest groups. Labor unions back the minimum wage because it prices disadvantaged workers out of the marketplace. Occupational licensing makes it harder for poor people to enter a variety of trades, such as driving a cab. Trade barriers to protect selected industries push up the cost of clothing, food, shoes, and a host of other goods. Antiquated building codes that guarantee construction jobs increase housing costs. Expansive government transfer programs enrich influential voting blocs—farmers, retirees, and the like—at the expense of the poor and middle class. And so on.

In a true market economy, those with the least influence can still gain access to economic opportunity. The more expansive the government controls, the more likely are concentrated interest groups to twist policy to their own ends, to the detriment of the most disadvantaged in society. This does not mean that capitalism is enough for a just and "Christian," society. Private mediating institutions, particularly associations, charities, and churches, are needed to play a critical role in helping those who, like the proverbial widows and orphans in the Old Testament, are unable to succeed in a market economy. Even welfare programs are not per se inconsistent with a generally free society, though they need to be better designed than the current system to avoid subsidizing illegitimacy and family break-up and discouraging work. And, in practice, such a goal may be impossible.

The Virtues of Capitalism

Respect for the virtues of capitalism is not limited to America's Religious Right. In the Pope's 1991 encyclical, *Centesimus Annus,* Catholic social teaching explicitly recognizes the benefits of a market system. The Pope's critique of Marxism is devastating: "The historical experience of socialist countries has sadly demonstrated that collectivism does not do away with alienation but rather increases it, adding to it a lack of basic necessities and economic inefficiency." In contrast, he praises capitalism, including its reliance on entrepreneurship and profits. "When a firm makes a profit," he wrote, "this means that productive factors have been properly employed and corresponding human needs have been duly satisfied." All told, he argues, "the free market is the most efficient instrument for utilizing resources and effectively responding to needs." He remains vitally concerned about the poor, however, and believes that capitalism cannot be the sum of society. He criticizes "consumerism" and advocates government intervention to ensure that "fundamental human needs" are not left unsatisfied. Finally, he writes that individual freedom needs an "ethical and religious" core.

Is capitalism Christian? No—it neither advances existing human virtues nor corrects ingrained personal vices; it merely reflects them. But socialism is less consistent with several Biblical tenets, for it exacerbates the worst of men's flaws. By divorcing effort from reward, stirring up covetousness and envy, and destroying the freedom that is a necessary precondition for virtue, it tears at the just social fabric that Christians should seek to establish. A Christian must still work hard to shed even a little of God's light in a capitalist society. But his task is likely to be much harder in a collectivist system.

The "Health Care Crisis" and the Morality of Capitalism

Charles D. Van Eaton

Charles Van Eaton is the Evert McCabe/UPS Professor of Economics and chairman of the department of economics at Hillsdale College. He also serves as a senior policy analyst for the Mackinac Center and an advisor to the Heartland Institute.

He writes a weekly syndicated column for the Hoiles Freedom Newspaper Group and has authored two landmark studies, "Privatization: Theory and Application for Michigan" (sponsored by the Michigan State Chamber Foundation) and "Revitalization of the American City: A Market Perspective for Detroit," which have become standard references on privatization for policy makers and municipal leaders throughout the nation.

Is the free marketplace the testing ground for morality in action? Does open competition lead to ruthless exploitation or to a better standard of living for all? These are important and complex questions that can be answered in a variety of ways. What I propose to do here is to answer them by examining what is widely regarded as one of the most troubling problems of the decade, the "health care crisis."

The Presumed Objective Problem in the Production of Health Care Services

First, a great deal needs to be said about how we came to believe that there is a "crisis." Health care costs are allegedly rising faster than other prices as measured by the Consumer Price Index, and, unless something is done, say the current Democratic administration and the Democratic Congress, there will be nothing but trouble ahead.

But health care is a service, and service prices are far more difficult to measure and index than goods prices. If one were to compare one service, say, higher education (which, like health care, employs individuals with significant human capital investment), with health care, one would find that health care costs have increased over the past two decades at a rate roughly equal to the cost of higher education. Is this too much? That is another issue, but seeing the issue in this way, rather than in the way it is routinely reported in the media, allows more light and less heat to shine on the problem.

The primary evidence that there is a crisis lies in the existence of 37 million persons without health insurance. How does one read this figure? Is it "37 million people who cannot afford insurance?" Is it "37 million people who are not getting health care?" Reading it either of these ways is to read it wrongly. Reading it correctly, we discover: The uninsured receive medical care by paying directly and by relying on private and public charity. Data reported by government economist Eugene Moyer shows that 67 percent of the uninsured are uninsured for less than year; they are predominately young—less than 30 years old—many are middle or upper class (48 percent in some reports) and 70 percent are employed. A study released by the Robert Wood Johnson Foundation shows that the uninsured's number of service visits with physicians and number of days of hospital care is not, when the subsidy factor of health insurance is taken into account, different in any statistically significant way, from the insured.

Another increasingly common allegation is that Americans are forced to spend more on health care than is necessary, and only government can solve this problem. But for the past seventeen years health care costs, adjusted for population and purchasing-power-parity, have been rising faster in Canada than in the United States. Canadian provincial governments are looking for ways to cut costs because the capacity to raise taxes is limited by the nation's "tax wall." Since the system is so politicized, health care workers are trying to convince citizens to block efforts to cut costs. Why?

Because they live off the system and do not want to see it cut. It is their income which is at stake.

Meanwhile, health costs are rising so rapidly in Western Europe that efforts are under way to curtail services and remove the shackles that now exist—i.e., to move away from centralized, government-run systems. In Germany, where the health care system is almost identical to the one President Clinton wants Congress to approve, health care spending rose faster during the decade of the 1980s than it did in the U.S.

But, say some observers, don't those nations that spend less on health care have more efficient systems? The fact that some countries have been able to *ration* health care successfully doesn't mean that they are running efficient systems. Japan spends far less per capita than America, but the average hospital stay in Japan is fifty days, compared to nine days in the U.S. That is not a sign of efficiency. And there is another problem with cross-cultural cost comparisons. Data analysis reveals, as one should expect, that health care is strongly income-elastic. Consequently, as income rises, the demand for health care should rise relatively more. Studies done by A. J. Culyer reveal that the significantly higher income level enjoyed by Americans (when expressed in purchasing power parity terms compared to other nations) accounts for 80 percent of the amount Americans spend on health care compared to other countries. For example, if the U.S. and Canada were exactly alike in all respects—including having identical health care delivery systems, on income-difference grounds alone per-capita spending in the U.S. would be $117 more than is spent in Canada.

Furthermore, University of Colorado economist Suzanne Tregarthen notes that the way we gather data overstates health care cost by as much as *43 percent;* the data do not account for "transactions costs"—the actual charges paid. Physicians discount up to 90 percent of their charges, yet this is not captured. Out-patient charges are noted on a per-day basis and are presumed to reflect old practices of keeping patients in the hospital. Once an outpatient procedure replaces conventional procedures, the new, lower cost charge for an outcome is not counted. Therefore, government numbers on health care simply don't add up.

The Anticapitalist Spirit that Animates the Current Debate on Health Care

The anticapitalist spirit that animates the current administration's and the Democratic-controlled Congress's approach to health care and to other economic issues is perhaps best represented by a recent statement made by Representative Robert Wise (D-WV): "The American myth is that a free market and laissez-faire will take care of health-care problem. It will not, and that has been clearly demonstrated."

Markets don't work? Is that what Representative Wise is suggesting? *Markets always work.* Whether or not they yield outcomes that satisfy some perception of perfection depends on the incentives that inform the system. As the late Nobel economist F.A. Hayek noted:

> The distribution of available resources between different uses, which is the *economic problem,* is no less a problem for society than for the individual, and, although the decision is not consciously made by anybody, the *competitive mechanism* does bring about some sort of solution.

F.A. Hayek also observed in his book, *The Fatal Conceit,* that when it becomes necessary to adapt to unknown circumstances where preferences may differ and knowledge is so diffused that no single person can hope to have access to all the information one would prefer to have, competition serves best because it is through competition that we learn to generate and assimilate information, respond to novel situations, and gradually overcome our inefficiency.

To repeat: Markets always work. Note how markets work within the legal and negotiating structure that currently operates in health care—a structure badly skewed by the fact that government directly (through Medicare and Medicaid) or indirectly (through the tax system) influences 95 percent of all health care spending (the amount covered by sources other than out-of-pocket payments by patients).

The anticapitalist spirit is also represented by the view that prices are relatively unimportant in influencing people's behavior. But prices *do* matter. At lower prices, as Martin Feldstein's research has shown, demand for health care becomes more elastic. Under third-party payment plans, the perceived price of health care to the insured rapidly approaches zero and quantity demanded reaches the point where the marginal utility of one more unit of health care is at or near hypothetical zero.

Health care spending has been rising because prices paid by patients have been falling. Over the past thirty years the share of income spent out-of-pocket on health care has actually declined—falling from 4 percent of total consumption in 1960 to 3.6 percent in 1990. At the same time, the amount spent from all sources has more than tripled—someone else is paying our bills! Consequently, quantity demanded outstrips the quantity that can be supplied at unchanged prices. Because the supply of health care is inelastic compared to demand, increases in subsidized demand result in mainly higher costs rather than in more services.

"But what about the uninsured?" say the anticapitalists. Don't they suffer disproportionately because of the free market? The response to this question is that the main source of higher spending on health care is not the free market but *government*, which now spends more than half our health care dollars. Because of third-party payers and government subsidies, the cost of health care is largely hidden from American families. With the failure of government to cover its agreed-upon share of service costs, e.g., in Medicare and Medicaid, costs are driven up and shifted. Other service costs must rise to cover the shortfall. Insurance costs rise and low-income workers may be priced out.

Because of third-party insurance and government subsidies, the most costly services are often the cheapest to patients. On average, patients pay 4.5 cents out of pocket for every dollar they spend on hospitals, but 68 cents out of every dollar they spend on pharmaceuticals. To patients, hospital therapy appears cheaper than drug therapy, although to society as a whole, the opposite may be true—the demands for more costly hospital services rise, costs rise, and insurance costs rise.

In 1990, government "spent" about $64 billion subsidizing private health insurance through the tax system. But the largest subsidies go to those who need them least—people who probably could and would purchase health insurance without subsidy. Current law penalizes people who purchase their own health insurance because they must do it with after-tax dollars. So, government spends about two dollars to obtain one dollar of real health services. If we moved to a totally government-run system as now prevails in Canada, health care spending as a percent of GDP would rise from the current 14 percent (itself based on questionable data) to 18 percent, unless we ration.

Further evidence of the anticapitalist spirit that establishes the terms of debate on health care comes from our First Lady, Mrs. Hillary Rodham Clinton. Speaking of immunizations for children, she says, "Unless you are willing to take on those who profit . . . you cannot provide the kind of universal immunization system that this country needs to have." And, she adds, "This nation has a patchwork, broken down health care system."

Mrs. Clinton fails to tell us that in half the states immunizations are free and that in all other states they are provided in public clinics for a purely nominal charge. Yet there is no greater parent participation in seeing that children are immunized when shots are free than there is in states where insurance or parents pay directly—even when payment is nominal. Does the First Lady not know this?

Does the First Lady not know that pharmaceutical companies must pay large sums (actually a tax) to a government-required fund for every vial of serum sold to cover liability and that this is not true in other countries? Does she not know that this tax on childhood vaccines exceeded the full price of such vaccines a decade ago?

While admitting that jobs will be lost under this health care plan, President Clinton argues that more jobs (200,000 in five years) will be lost without the plan. He goes on to argue that more jobs will be gained, without saying how many more jobs. In response to the editors' concerns about federal mandates requiring small employers to cover insurance costs, Vice President Al Gore declared in the March 30, 1993 issue of the *Wall Street Journal:* "You want to argue about mandates by arguing that small business employees would not take health insurance if they had to pay a share. This is way off the mark!"

But who's really off the mark on this point? While admitting that the administration's health care plan calls for employers to pay up to 8 percent of payroll into mandated plans for a government-determined health care plan, one wonders if the vice president has felt any moral necessity to consider the detailed study done by Baruch College economists June and David O'Neill. This careful study concludes that this feature of the plan will translate directly into higher labor costs and cost up to 3.1 million jobs. The lost jobs will be concentrated in the restaurant, retail trade, and construction industries. Does Gore not know that these industries cannot easily shift costs and that they are critical entry-level industries? Now, who is it that's "off the mark"?

The Clintons, Gore, and others in the current administration have also attacked providers. They have said that rising health costs are the fault of "profiteers" in the health insurance industry, and they plan to "get tough." For some reason they have chosen not to figure out why the top twenty health insurance companies have lost money writing health insurance in seven of the last ten years. This is not the kind of spirit that points to a solution of the health care problem; it is the kind of spirit that itself becomes a problem.

The Myth of "Perfect Competition"

The usual textbook definition of "perfect competition" assumes the following:

Many sellers. Each seller is so small relative to the market that no one can affect price by any action he chooses to take and, consequently, each seller becomes a *price taker.*

Homogenous product. No seller can effectively distinguish his product from that of any rival.

Perfect information. Information is known to all, with the result that every buyer can always know where the lowest price is, and every seller can always know where the highest price is. There is always and everywhere one price for every homogenous product.

No barriers to entry and exit. Anyone can become a seller at any time under equal conditions.

In "The Meaning of Competition," F. A. Hayek noted that there is nothing in such a model that "tells us anything about the process by which data are adjusted so that anything which could be called 'equilibrium' might emerge." In a word, the conventional theory of "perfect competition" assumes away the market process it is presumed to contain. What is ignored is this: Competition is the dynamic process that discovers new ways of doing things and forces the abandonment of old ways of doing things. Competition is first and foremost a discovery procedure.

What, then, is the correct way to understand competition? Competition should be understood as a process of continuous rivalry; a process that compels discovery—a process that generates and retrieves information—a process that destroys the old to make room for the creation of the new. Essential to this process is a system of prices that provides signals to all parties to all transactions—signals that in turn provide information to the human actors who employ them. Such prices are not "equilibrium prices" in the sense in which such prices might be expected to prevail in the textbook model of perfect competition, but they *are* prices, and the coordination they make possible is not the general equilibrium set so loved by the neoclassical economist but the equilibrium that exists in the real world.

The Myth of "Managed Competition": The Jackson Hole Health Care Plan

The absence of some presumed "equilibrium set" of prices—in the sense that the cost of health care is rising faster than some statistical index number of prices in general—is one reason liberal and sometimes even conservative groups say we have a "health care crisis" in this country that must be solved by the creation of a new "market" that will yield a better process of "competition" than that which currently exists.

These are the groups that advocate "managed competition," which they claim is really nothing more than another term for a kind of general dynamic system of rivalry among health care providers and, therefore, competition. The most well known is the so-called "Jackson Hole Group," associated with Paul Ellwood, M.D., and Alain C. Enthoven, Ph.D., a Stanford University economist and former defense undersecretary in the Johnson administration. Together with others, their first draft of a national managed competition system bears the title, "The 21st Century American Health System."

This system would divide the health care delivery system into regional blocks of group purchasers and group providers. Companies and individuals would no longer buy traditional coverage directly from insurance companies. Instead, federally sanctioned purchasing cooperatives—one to a region—would negotiate with groups of health care providers. Each of these provider groups would offer a pre-priced package of services, and consumers would pick the package that best fits their needs.

Each health plan, which would be organized and managed by insurance companies, physicians or others, would group together providers, and market forces would yield a price for services. One price would have to prevail for all under one kind of coverage in each region. Consumers would get an audit from a nonprofit agency that rated each plan for price and quality. Although private practice would could continue to exist, many believe HMOs would come to prevail because traditional fee-for-service would become too expensive. Doctors in HMOs would tend to be on salary.

Dr. Ellwood believes "99 percent" of the insurance companies would be wiped out because they only know how to be insurance companies, not "care managers." Under managed care, insurance companies would organize and manage the health plans, which would be made up of hospitals, physicians, laboratories, and other types of providers. Such arrangements, called Accountable Health Plans, could also be organized by hospitals, groups of physicians, and others.

In its original proposal, the Jackson Hole Group argued that limits should be set on the tax-exempt amounts that a firm could use for offering employees better health benefits. By driving down the amount employers and individuals would be willing to pay, the cost of an HMO's bid to serve would fall. However, critics in the administration don't want to eliminate the tax-exempt nature of premiums paid by employers.

Is this kind of "managed competition" really just like open competition? The answer is no. *The Jackson Hole plan is nothing more than a government-sanctioned cartel.* This is not competition in any sense of the word; it is an invitation for special interest groups to find a place for themselves within the cartel while doing all they politicially can to keep others out.

The Myth of "Managed Competition": The Clinton Health Care Plan

The stated goal of the Clinton health care plan, which has many of the same features as the Jackson Hole plan, is to require employers to *guarantee* a comprehensive package of benefits to all Americans while at the same time cut the growth rate of health care spending in half. High quality, low cost, full access—these are the goals.

Here, however, are the actual details: There will be an "organized delivery system" put in place designed to provide "cradle to grave" medical services under one umbrella organization. Regional buying organizations would be created and all individuals and employers must pay into them. These alliances would then accept bids from provider groups, and would collect money annually from employers and individuals and contract with health plans that meet federal standards. The alliances would then publish information on the various HMOs, etc., and would issue "quality performance reports." Moreover, the alliances would have to approve all marketing materials that health plans send out and could limit the number of plans that can operate. The alliances could also bar providers from charging more than what is specified on published fee schedules. New bureaucracies would be set up in every state to limit enrollment in alternative plans and, in some cases, approve how much a physician could charge for services.

A National Health Board, appointed by the president, would set strict budgets in the form of "premium targets," which would cap the amount private health insurers could charge. The budgets would be unbending. No one health-provider organization could continue to contract with the alliance if its charges exceeded the plan's targets. Ira Magaziner, Mrs. Clinton's chief adviser, claims the national board would only function like a "board of directors" without much staff. And the entire administration persistently argues that targets are not price controls; they are only devices to force providers to be efficient. But, in May of 1993, Mrs. Clinton told a group of senators that the administration will look for "voluntary price restraints" within the health industry. And, of course, the program would include federal authority to impose a rigid set of restraints if the industry failed to keep costs below the "agreed-upon" level.

The Clinton health care plan doesn't stop there either. A national advisory council for medical schools would be established to determine the "appropriate number" of training slots for each medical speciality. White House advisers say that many of the controls would be in place only as a "back up" in case the plan's efforts to spur markets were not as effective as anticipated. However, Duke University economist Frank Sloan, who specializes in the economics of health care, argues that the controls will quickly become the driving force because "that's where the action is."

Max Gammon, a practicing physician in London, tells us where "managed competition" in British health care has moved and how it has changed the character of medical practice since "the action" has forced political ambitions to take precedence over everything else. In early 1993, Gammon reports, it was announced that more than one million patients were waiting for hospital admission, and the number of those waiting for more than a year was rising. A number of patients no longer appear on the waiting list simply because there are no beds to accommodate them. To save costs, incredibly, hospitals are being closed.

The historical on-the-spot role of the hospital "sister" (ward nurse) has declined, too, as sisters have learned that the real money is in administration. From cleaners and porters to physicians, increasing numbers of National Health Service staff members, irrespective of their designated functions, have been spending increasing amounts of time in centrally prescribed activities not directly related to patient care, leaving fewer and less experienced personnel for that purpose. In 1948, when the government first began to take over health care, there were 350,000 staff for 480,000 beds. In 1991, there were 800,000 staff for 260,000 beds, yet wards were being closed for lack of nurses and physicians.

Proponents of the Clinton plan pooh-pooh any comparison to the British experience. They insist that they have kept a significant number of market features; but critics contend that there is enough regulation to undercut any market forces that might possibly survive implementation of the plan. Uwe Reinhardt of Princeton argues, for instance, that "The Clinton plan will divert income from people who lay hands on people to people who supervise doctors." And it will also divert more power from individuals to the federal government; if states failed to "comply with federal standards," the secretary of the U.S. Treasury could impose a payroll tax on all resident employers.

The Clinton health care plan is not one of government-sanctioned private cartels; it is one of government cartels. One is reminded of the early debates over the possibility of rational economic decisions under socialism—the Lange-Taylor response to Ludwig von Mises: "The socialist state can reach the right equilibrium prices more quickly than markets because the Central Planning Board would have much wider knowledge than would prevail in markets." Inherent in the Clinton health care plan is the assumption that a central health planning board would have wider knowledge than any other group or any individuals and would set the terms of the debate. This is the same view shared by early socialists, who argued that government would always "know best," and that people are not to be trusted on their own.

Interestingly enough, it was another managed competition advocate, Dr. Ellwood, who attacked the Clinton plan in the August 10, 1993 issue of the *Wall Street Journal:* "The White House seems not to understand that its job is to help the private sector do the job. Instead it focuses its energy on government strategies for managing health care costs and on the creation of quasi-government purchasing pools with the power to impose regulatory restraints on health care providers."

Open Competition: The Best Economic and Moral Solution to the "Health Care Crisis"

President Clinton argues that his health care plan will reduce the national deficit by $91 billion. There is an interesting history to this presumption. When Medicare finally passed in 1965, Representative Phil Burton (D-CA) expressed the sentiment of many in the "Great Society" when he said, "I am equally certain that before many years Congress will choose to extend comprehensive medical coverage as a matter of right to every man, woman, and child in the country." At that time, Medicare cost only $3 billion a year, and its cost was expected to rise to a maximum of $12 billion by 1990. The hospital cost component was estimated to rise to $9 billion. In 1990, in fact, the hospital cost was $63 billion, and the overall cost of this federal boondoggle was over $120 billion—ten times higher than the original estimate.

Given this history, it is not surprising that even as President Clinton claims huge cost reductions for his plan, the Congressional Budget Office estimates that it will increase costs by $328 billion a year. What has become popularly known among free market economists as Gammon's Law also applies: All bureaucracies exist to suck in resources while emitting less and less. They become fiscal "black holes." Why would any rational person expect the bureaucracy that would emerge to operate the Clinton health care plan to be different?

Under the Clinton health care plan, doctors will lose their freedom. They will become essentially employees of the state—simply another part of the growing number of government employees; a group that now comprises the largest portion of U.S. unionized labor.

Under the Clinton health care plan, families and individuals will lose their freedom. Real markets and real empowerment can only occur when families and individuals are enabled to buy their own coverage with medical care savings accounts and tax credits. The more a person is subsidized, the more is spent. Medicare spends $5,446 per person; Medicaid spends $3,565. Large groups spend $1,511; individuals spend $711—and that includes $10 billion spent for "free care."

The additional problem with all this is that advocates of managed competition want government to manage it. Without waiting for the market to work, they have already decided that *everyone* should be in a managed care program. In addition, whatever they may choose to call it, they also want price-fixing for health insurance premiums. And they advocate such heavy regulation of the health insurance industry that for all practical purposes insurers would be forced out of the insurance business as traditionally understood and into the business of managed care. This is like insisting that an auto insurance company go into the business of operating body shops.

What I mean by "open competition," or the "competitive order," is almost the opposite of what is often referred to as "ordered competition." As Hayek noted, the purpose of a competitive order is to make competition work; that of ordered competition is almost always to restrict the effectiveness of competition. Once enacted, the Clinton plan would be no different from socialism because it relies on "ordered competition," and it bears no relationship to competition properly understood.

Worse yet, it would help destroy the moral foundations of our economy, since all moral issues are issues of personal responsibility within freely chosen communities. Is this assertion true? Consider these words—the last spoken to a people who had once been slaves but who were now free: "Today, choose whom you will serve, whether the gods your fathers served in the region beyond the River. . . . But as for me and my house, we will serve the Lord." Tough choice? Maybe, but free people are free precisely because they are able to choose, even to choose the wrong things.

Government intervention, which, by definition, must be based on coercion and must deny the individual in favor of the collective, can never be moral. It might yield "good" outcomes, but these outcomes are not the product of morals, they are the product of pure luck. Government is not reason. It is not eloquence. It *is* force. And force, like fire, is what George Washington called "a dangerous servant and a fearful master."

The Evangelical Kaleidoscope: Economics, Politics, and Social Justice

Michael Cromartie

Formerly a consultant to the U.S. Justice Department and a special assistant to Charles W. Colson at Prison Fellowship Ministries, Michael Cromartie is currently a research fellow in Protestant studies and the director of the Evangelical Studies Project with the Ethics and Public Policy Center in Washington, D.C.

He has written numerous articles and reviews and with Richard John Neuhaus is coeditor of *Piety and Politics: Evangelicals and Fundamentalists Confront the World* (now in its fifth printing and named by *Eternity* magazine as one of the 25 best books published in 1988). He also is editor of numerous books from the Ethics and Public Policy Center, including *Might and Right After the Cold War: Can Foreign Policy Be Moral?* (1993), *No Longer Exiles: The Religious New Right in American Politics* (1993), *Peace Betrayed? Essays on Pacificism and Politics* (1990), and *Gaining Ground: New Approaches to Poverty and Dependency* (1985). In addition, Mr. Cromartie is widely recognized as an authority on religious affairs by the national media and has appeared on such programs as NPR's "All Things Considered," CNN's "Prime News," and CBN News.

For many political pundits and observers, American evangelicals represent a mass movement of cultural dinosaurs and their religious views are what H.L. Mencken called a "childish theology" for "halfwits," "yokels," the "anthropoid rabble," or the "gaping primates of the upland valleys." And that was just for starters. Mencken said in 1925 that Christendom may be defined as that part of the world where if anyone stands up and solemnly swears he is a Christian, all his auditors will laugh.

Well, to the bewilderment of many, the gaping primates from the upland valleys are still very much with us and they have become a very large voting bloc. Mencken said this in 1924: "Heave an egg out a Pullman train window and you will hit a Fundamentalist almost anywhere in the United States today." If Mencken were living today he might put a different spin on it: "Heave an egg out a window anywhere on Capitol Hill today and you will likely hit an evangelical political activist." There was a time when political involvement by evangelicals was seen as worldly, or even sinful, activity. Now, political celibacy, if you will, is considered an abdication of Christian responsibility. The change has resulted in American evangelicals creating a lively debate among themselves on economics, politics, and capitalism. This debate has a history and my task here is to give an overview of this debate as it has transpired over the last five decades.

That Christians should be involved in economic, political and social concerns has become a foregone conclusion. As one theologian has put it, the effort to validate such involvement "is tantamount to a statistical survey demonstrating that all husbands are married!" Christian economic, political, and social activity has always existed. What is new is this huge voting bloc called the "Religious Right," which is composed of millions of evangelical and fundamentalist Christians who are relatively new arrivals on the political scene.

A friend of mine who is a veteran writer for the *Washington Post* remarked to me after the election of Bill Clinton that the political involvement of evangelicals "is history; they are finished." He went on to say that the recent book I edited called *No Longer Exiles: The Religious New Right in American Politics* should have been entitled simply *Exiled!* But I replied to my friend at the *Post* that the title could actually have been called *Revived* in light of the new target-rich environment to shoot at with the current administration in power. In 1993 Pat Robertson's Christian Coalition held its national convention in Washington with 2,000 participants from almost every state in the country. The extensive coverage of their meeting gave every indication that they are still a major political force to be taken seriously by leaders in both parties.

Defining Different Evangelical Groups

It is important that I define some terms. Some people in the press, sounding dumbfounded and shocked, will periodically call me at my office and want to know who are all these people, where did they all come from, and what is the core of their complaint. One reporter called me and asked the following in one breathless question: "What," she asked, "is the difference between fundamentalists and evangelicals, between pentecostals and Baptists, between charismatics and fundamentalists, between Jerry Falwell, Pat Robertson, Billy Graham, and *Sojourners* magazine?" (I think I said, "Could you repeat the question?")

Defining these terms has become increasingly complex within American religious historiography. But let me try to explain them anyway. Protestant evangelicalism is a conservative theological tradition that is devoted to the classical Protestant doctrine of salvation through justification by faith alone. The Bible is seen as the only infallible Word of God and the final authority for the believer in all matters of faith and practice. Evangelicals believe in the priesthood of all believers and the fundamental obligation to preach the Christian message to all people. Evangelicals do not come from a single historical source. The distinctive features of their doctrinal beliefs are rooted in: (1) the Protestant Reformation of the sixteenth century; (2) the evangelical revivals and awakenings associated with George Whitefield, Jonathan Edwards, and John Wesley in the eighteenth century; and (3) the conservative theological movement that grew out of the "fundamentalist-modernist" controversy in the first three decades of the twentieth century. What, then, is a fundamentalist, and what is the difference between a fundamentalist and an evangelical? I like historian George Marsden's definition: "A fundamentalist is an evangelical who is mad about something." What he means simply is that while evangelicals and fundamentalists have similar doctrinal beliefs, fundamentalists tend to be more militant and legalistic about it. There is a sharper "edge" and tone to much of the rhetoric of fundamentalists, which results in there being different stylistic approaches to the wider culture.

What surprises most observers is just how diverse evangelical intellectual opinions are on economic and political issues. It is commonplace to believe that theologically conservative Protestants are all conservative economically and politically. This is not always the case. Historian Timothy L. Smith has written about what he calls the "evangelical mosaic or kaleidoscope," which includes not only a diversity of denominations but also Christians from the political right, left, and center. In 1985 the *Wall Street Journal* carried a front-page report entitled "Radical Evangelicals Are Gaining Influence Protesting U.S. Foreign Policy." The article described the "growing and increasingly influential group of evangelicals whose conservative theology has led to radical— some would say leftist—political action." So evangelicals are by no means monolithic in their political views. While they have largely maintained an alliance with political conservatism, they have a liberal/left wing contingent that has an influence that far exceeds its numbers.

At a small meeting I attended of evangelical economists, philosophers, and biblical scholars of diverse political persuasions several years ago, a leading philosopher (who at the time would have considered himself a member of the evangelical left) begrudgingly admitted after two days of debate that free market capitalism was more efficient in producing wealth and, as a result, in helping the poor. However, while waving his arms in the air, he protested: "Okay, I agree with everything that has been said here the last two days about the efficiency of capitalism, but I want to go on record as saying that I still don't like Disneyland and Disney World!" "That is interesting," replied an economist from the University of Virginia—"it used to be that the socialist critique of capitalism was that it just didn't work—now you are saying that it works too well!" The philosopher was not so dissatisfied by the economic results of the market economy as by the capitalist *culture* that accompanied it, a culture that is sometimes characterized by narcissism, lawlessness, and excessive materialism.

The Proper Relationship Between Faith, Economics, and Politics

For evangelical Christians, the debate concerning the proper relationship of religious faith to economics and politics has become an urgent issue. Evangelicals engage in the business and legislative worlds now not only as participants, but, in the minds of many people at least, they engage as defendants. *What* many people in the press ask, are these people trying to do? Some in the press used to wonder aloud whether the involvement of evangelicals should be even taken seriously. They wonder no more: The Huge market and voting bloc that evangelicals and fundamentalists represent is taken seriously, at least by the Republican Party. Many commentators thought the rise of conservative Protestant involvement was only a momentary aberration in American public life—a blip on the national screen—and that it would soon go away. *They thought wrong.* I now advise my friends in the press that they had better start reading theology and attending evangelical churches if they want to stay ahead of their colleagues in covering this story!

For over fifty years in this century, a large sector of conservative evangelical social thought had been influenced by a pessimistic form of theological dispensationalism and a pietistic individualism that looked with disdain on efforts to improve social conditions and political structures. They had originally believed that the process of secularization was simply irreversible, and this pessimism was reinforced by their theology. But this had not always been the case.

Up until the Scopes trial in Dayton, Tennessee in 1925 (where a biology teacher, John Scopes, challenged a Tennessee law that banned the teaching of Darwinism), evangelicals had aggressively addressed almost every major economic, political, and social question in American public life. At the Scopes trial, William Jennings Bryan defended the Tennessee law and won, but his performance against ACLU lawyer Clarence Darrow was so embarrassing that it was ridiculed in the press and he, and fundamentalism, lost in the court of public opinion. This made it increasingly difficult to take conservative Protestantism seriously, and it caused millions of evangelical and fundamentalist Christians to retreat from society. The pessimistic theological worldview described above gave them religious reasons for doing so.

But there were other reasons for this withdrawal from society. In theological circles there was a controversial debate surrounding the redefinition of the Christian message led by a leading liberal Protestant thinker named Walter Rauschenbusch. He had written a very important book called *A Theology for the Social Gospel* (1917). Rauschenbusch wanted to challenge conservative Protestants for what he felt was an individualistic approach to personal salvation that neglected social reform. His concept of the social gospel was an attempt to enlarge and intensify the old message of salvation. He said: "The individualistic gospel has taught us to see the sinfulness of every human heart and has inspired us with faith in the willingness and power of God to save every human soul that comes to him. But it has not given us an adequate understanding of the sinfulness of the social order and its share in the sins of all individuals within it." Rauschenbusch redefined sin to mean essentially selfishness, and he blamed capitalism for encouraging greed and the pursuit of private gain at the expense of those in need. Capitalism, he argued, "impressed a materialistic spirit on our whole civilization" and to renounce it in favor of socialism was to "step out of the Kingdom of Evil into the Kingdom of God." His influence was profound, and his redefinition of the Christian meaning of salvation (which was more of a social message than a personal one) can still be seen in many of our mainline Protestant churches today. And, as you can imagine, evangelical and fundamentalist leaders were not pleased with the message of Walter Rauschenbusch.

The Challenge of the Social Gospel

Their reaction might be summed up by looking at two very different responses to the challenge of what became known as the social gospel. Princeton theologian Charles Erdman, in an essay entitled, "The Church and Socialism," expressed his deep concern about the social gospel movement. He emphatically stated that it was dangerous to identify the Christian message with any economic theory or political system. But he was particularly concerned with the attempts by many to "identify socialism with Christianity." He cautioned that socialism could become a substitute religion and one that was, moreover, hostile to Christianity. He also warned that, while "the strength of socialism consists largely in its protest against existing social wrongs to which the Church is likewise opposed," these wrongs can "be finally righted only by the universal rule of Christ."

The strongest response to the growing social gospel movement was constructed by the Presbyterian fundamentalist Carl McIntire in his book, *The Rise of the Tyrant: Controlled Economy vs. Private Enterprise* (1945). McIntire argued that capitalism, free enterprise, and individual liberty were "grounded in the moral nature of God." The Bible, he said, "teaches private enterprise and the capitalistic system, not as a by-product or as some sideline, but as the very foundation of society itself in which men are to live and render an account of themselves to God." McIntire even insisted that many of the major figures in biblical history, including Abraham and Moses, had been capitalists.

We should note here, then, the diversity of evangelical and fundamentalist opinions concerning capitalism, and their varied responses to the challenge of the social gospel movement. It is clear, says Craig Gay of Regent College (in Canada), that "somewhere in between Charles Erdman and Carl McIntire a theological line had been crossed. While Erdman had maintained the impossibility of identifying Christ with any particular political-economic system, McIntire had all but equated modern industrial capitalism with the will of God in the world." This form of theological reductionism is ironic because it collapses economic and political concerns to a "this-worldly" level in an attempt to make the Christian faith relevant to the economic debate—the very charge leveled at leaders of the social gospel movement in its promotion of socialism. So the irony is striking—and as one observer has noted wryly, "there are many ironies in the fire" when discussing this topic.

A New Christian Apologetic

In the early 1940s there were a number of more moderate fundamentalists who began to question the militant and confrontational style of fundamentalists like McIntire. They became known as "neo-evangelicals" and their leading spokesman was Carl F. H. Henry. In 1947 Carl Henry wrote a very influential book called *The Uneasy Conscience of Modern Fundamentalism*. It was a clarion call for evangelicals to confront the modern world with a Christian apologetic that was both intellectually respectable and socially responsible. According to Henry, the theological separatism of fundamentalism had led to a separation from cultural and social responsibilities and to a mistaken disengagement from the important issues of the day. This backlash reaction to the social gospel movement had created an almost complete avoidance of social programs and issues for fear of resembling the social gospel. This divorce between Christian proclamation and Christian compassion, Henry argued, was an abandonment of the clear mandates given by Scripture and church history. Henry condemned this tragic development in the strongest terms. He agreed that although capitalism was a superior economic system, there was no excuse for neglecting the clear biblical teachings regarding the duty and obligations of evangelicals towards social and political problems.

Making these connections between faith and politics was quite novel and, at the time, controversial among evangelicals. Neo-evangelical leaders like Henry, E.J. Carnell, and Harold Ockenga had their persistent critics among separatist fundamentalists on their right. But critics began to form on their left as well. The many issues and questions raised by the political activism and social turbulence of the 1960s caused a further reexamination of evangelicism's often cozy link to the establishment status quo.

"Social Justice" and Statist Solutions

A new younger generation of "radical evangelicals" felt that Henry and the neo-evangelicals had not gone far enough in their critique of capitalism and social injustices in American society. They accused the mainstream evangelical establishment of being "ideologically captive" to a "decadent American capitalist culture."

The founding of the magazines *The Other Side* in 1965 and *Post American* in 1971 (renamed *Sojourners* in 1974) created forums for an ongoing critique of what the editors saw as a "truncated gospel" that neglected to attend to the abundance of biblical passages exhorting believers to seek justice for the oppressed and care for the poor. Jim Wallis, the editor of the radical evangelical magazine *Sojourners,* said in 1971 that "we have become disillusioned, alienated, and angered by an American system that we regard as oppressive; a society whose values are corrupt and destructive. We have unmasked the American Dream by exposing the American nightmare.... [O]ur ethical revolt against systemic injustice, militarism, and the imperialism of a 'power elite' is accompanied by our protest of a technocratic society and a materialistic profit-culture where human values are out of place." (Walter Rauschenbusch, call your office and meet Jim Wallis.)

Some of these pleas for compassion to the poor and the oppressed corrected a prior imbalance in evangelicalism's history. However, such calls for social justice on behalf of the poor and oppressed always looked for statist solutions to these intractable problems without any consideration that the state might make matters worse. I want to emphasize that within the evangelical academic community (and the larger religious community as well) there are some very strong differences regarding just what "social justice" is and who is ultimately responsible for maintaining it.

The early impact of these radical evangelical magazines was significant, as they further pricked evangelicals' "uneasy conscience" on issues such as racism, poverty, and social injustice. And their writers and editors played a vital role in the drafting of a landmark statement in 1973 called the "Chicago Declaration of Evangelical Social Concern." In Chicago some fifty evangelical leaders gathered for a two-day workshop that culminated in a significant statement on social responsibility.

The document received considerable attention in the press and was drafted and signed by moderate evangelicals such as Carl Henry and radical evangelicals such as Ronald Sider (who had convened the meeting) and Jim Wallis, editor of *Sojourners*. The statement emphasized that God requires his people to be loving, just, and abounding in mercy, but "we have not demonstrated the love of God to those suffering social abuses" and "have not proclaimed or demonstrated his justice to an unjust American society."

The "Chicago Declaration" set the tone and themes for much that was to be written subsequently about evangelical politics, economics, and social concern. Along with the important publication of a book called *Rich Christians in an Age of Hunger* by Ronald Sider, the Declaration initiated a vigorous discussion on the need for evangelicals to take the admonitions in the books of Amos and Jeremiah seriously as they consider the concerns for fulfilling the Great Commission. It also helped initiate a lively interaction of different Christian approaches to social ethics and sparked a healthy debate among, for instance, Anabaptist ethicists and Reformed political philosophers. And with the growth of the "health and wealth" gospel preached by many televangelists, radical evangelical writers sharpened dull consciences by calling their fellow Christians to simpler lifestyles, wiser stewardship, and compassion for the victims of racism and other forms of social and political injustice.

The Nation magazine wrote in 1985 that "the only left left is the religious left." One of the energizing forces of the religious left has been the publications and leadership of the radical evangelicals. While statistically small in numbers, the influence of the radical evangelicals, or the evangelical left, has been far greater than they are often credited for being. If nothing else, they serve as a "home" to run to for many intelligent mainstream evangelicals who are put off by the rhetoric of the "Religious Right."

But assessing the impact of the radical evangelicals is complex. Despite their success in awakening the evangelical social conscience in the early stages, their magazines are now more influential among left-wing Catholics and liberal Protestants, whose own memberships have been declining rapidly. Once thought to be the wave of future evangelical social thought, popular support for radical evangelical magazines has diminished significantly. Some commentators have found them to be strident, predictable and almost mirror images in tone to reactionary fundamentalists in their moralistic posturing. While it may be bracingly stimulating to hurl prophetic warnings toward the powers that be, it must be sobering when it appears that the only people paying attention are the directors of the "Prophetic Justice Unit" of the National Council of Churches. Even so, they still make some important contributions to public dialogue (by serving as a social conscience for many), but their marginalization has caused them to become, according to political scientist Robert Booth Fowler, an "opposition without teeth."

Reading their publications over the years, one gets the impression that they simply have never seen any enemies to their left. Of course, it is hard to see enemies to your left when the only people you read on economics and politics are on the left! Judging from what has been written in some radical evangelical publications, the chief source of injustice and global conflict in the world has always, and only, been America. Their motto, as one wag put it recently, is to "blame America first, early, and often." The number of subscribers to their magazines has plunged in the last several years, and this should not be surprising: One has to wonder why they do not know that readers tire of receiving moral and political direction from persons who incessantly tell them that the nation in which they live *is* the evil empire. One does not have to be a "God and country" civil religionist to find this inability to make political distinctions somewhat skewed. But distinctions between political and economic systems have to be drawn and sometimes very sharply. Yet, the writers on the evangelical left often give the clear impression that greed is peculiar *only* to capitalism. This, as Max Weber once said, is simply "a kindergarten notion."

The New Christian Right

Interestingly enough, the biggest growth of evangelical political activity did not come as a result of reading passionate pronouncements in radical evangelical books and magazines or from reading declarations from Chicago. Edward Dobson, a former special assistant to the Reverend Jerry Falwell, has said that Falwell realized how much potential there was to influence the political process in 1976, when, on his national television program, he criticized President Jimmy Carter for giving an interview to *Playboy* magazine. Much to his surprise, Falwell soon received a call from the president's special assistant, Jody Powell, asking that he refrain from making such comments. "Back off," Powell said to him. Falwell (who in the past has called himself both a fundamentalist and an evangelical) was startled to find that what he said had caused such concern in the White House. He came to perceive this incident as his "initial baptism" in the world of politics.

Many members of the evangelical right had similar triggering experiences, on a personal level, which left them obliged to become politically involved, which was something they had not been inclined to do previously, largely for theological reasons. The original priority of their leaders was not so much to persuade others of their views as it was to sensitize other evangelicals, fundamentalists, and charismatics to become involved in public issues that concerned them. It was not an easy task, since, as I have pointed out, many had been taught for decades that such activity was irrelevant and "of the world." But increasing pressures from a number of sectors caused this wing of the evangelical movement to feel, as sociologist Steve Bruce says in *The Rise and Fall of the New Christian Right* that they "were not getting their due" but could "if they organized to claim it." And organize they did. Their effective use of television and direct mail, the declining membership of liberal denominations, and the increasing membership of evangelical denominations gave them confidence and combined to make political involvement appear to be a promising and worthwhile endeavor.

What stirred them most was a sense that various Supreme Court decisions were giving increasing power to the opponents of traditional Christian virtues. They became engaged in what Harvard professor Nathan Glazer has called a "defensive offensive" against what they saw as an aggressive imposition of secular views on American society, including their own private communities of faith. The emergence of the Religious Right marked the beginning of a process that Carl Henry later described as the "hijacking of the evangelical jumbo jet while establishment leaders hesitated to forge an aggressive public program."

In due course they themselves began to be accused of "imposing their views" and "forcing their beliefs" on the community. But was this really the case? According to Harvard professor Nathan Glazer:

> Abortion was not a national issue until the Supreme Court, in 1973, set national standards for state laws. It did *not* become an issue because evangelicals and fundamentalist wanted to *strengthen* prohibitions against abortion, but because liberals wanted to abolish them.... Pornography in the 1980s did *not* become an issue because evangelicals and fundamentalists wanted to *ban* D.H. Lawrence, James Joyce, or even Henry Miller, but because in the 1960s and 1970s under-the-table pornography moved to the top of the newsstands. Prayer in the schools did *not* become an issue because evangelicals and fundamentalists wanted to introduce new prayers or sectarian prayers—but because the Supreme Court ruled against *all* prayers. Freedom for religious schools became an issue *not* because of any legal effort to expand their scope—but because the IRS and various state authorities tried to impose restrictions on them that private schools had not faced before.

This imposition of a liberal ethos by what many social scientists have called the "new class elites" (made up of newspaper journalists, television producers and commentators, and the "knowledge class" from the universities) is what aroused many previously apolitical and socially indifferent fundamentalists and evangelicals to action. While many evangelicals have always found plenty to complain about in the wider culture, the rapid changes in American society during the 1960s-1970s sent shock waves through their community. Sociologist Steve Bruce has pointed out that "Conservative Protestants of the 1950s were offended by girls smoking in public. In the late 1960s girls were to be seen on news film dancing naked at open-air rock concerts." In short, a cultural shift had occurred between Dwight Eisenhower's America and the America of the 1960s-1970s.

As a result, millions of fundamentalists and evangelicals have come to feel that they live in a hostile environment that is suffering from a moral and cultural nervous breakdown. "Enough is enough" is their cry. They no longer need convincing, by radical evangelicals, or anyone else for that matter, that the Scriptures have much to say about the proper relationship of private belief and public concern. Their agenda is not centrally focused on economic policies but more on abortion, pornography, homosexual rights, crime, and the breakdown of American families. Their political and economic instincts are conservative: Like many Americans they are concerned with the ever-expanding encroachments of our modern Leviathan.

Their political impact has been substantial, although controversial. The Religious Right is most effective in "preparing the ground" for conservative candidates: They register voters and spend money on general "sensitizing campaigns" or, to borrow a phrase from the left, "consciousness raising." According to television exit polls, they voted overwhelmingly for Ronald Reagan in 1980, at least 80 percent of evangelicals backed President Reagan's re-election in 1984, and in 1988, 79 percent of evangelicals supported President Bush. In 1992, disappointment with President Bush, the Ross Perot candidacy, and the presence of two Southern Baptists on the Democratic ticket caused their votes to be more spread out: 62 percent of evangelicals voted for

Bush, 25 percent voted for Clinton, and 19 percent voted for Ross Perot.

Sometimes the political rhetoric of some in the Religion Right reminds one of the careless and strident language of fundamentalists from earlier in this century. Some evangelicals, being relatively new to the transactions of politics, do not realize that politics requires the art of prudent and principled compromise: In a fallen world where public policy disputes have to be hammered out with nonbelievers, sometimes one has to give a little to get anything. But some evangelicals are purists who would rather alienate than cooperate. They have sometimes been reluctant to join coalitions—the very brick and mortar of electoral victories—because they seek a public policy *certainty* that is next to impossible to achieve among persons who, though they agree on a particular policy, are working from different presuppositions. Some evangelicals have been divisive and have used unnecessarily strident language toward their opponents—and even toward some of their natural allies.

But this has begun to change in recent years, as their leadership has come to realize that even the most prudent Christian sometimes has to make choices in the political realm between "relative goods" and "lesser evils." Our duties are shaped, not by all the choices we wish we had, but by the choices that we in fact have. Evangelicals must reflect on normative ideals in the face of real concrete situations. Evangelical ethics must always be applied, adapted, and compared to the existing alternatives and approximated in accordance with the available options.

An Historic Tradition of Involvement

It is strange that 20th century evangelical Christians would have ever needed to be convinced that they should be concerned about economic, political, and social problems. Their spiritual forebears always had been. Historian Grant Wacker has pointed out that "evangelicals, seeking to be the moral custodians of the culture have always known how to play political hardball when the prayer meeting let out."

Their compassion and fervor animated the campaigns against the slave trade and child labor in England, and, one could argue, were the basis of most reform initiatives of the early 19th century.

The intermingling of Christian faith with economic, political, and social concerns was always a part of our country's history. The claim that the faith of American Christians should always be an intensely private affair between the individual and God would have been news to such diverse persons as the Pilgrims, John Winthrop, Jonathan Edwards, Abraham Lincoln, the abolitionists, fifteen generations of the black church, civil rights leaders, and anti-war activists. Religious values have always been a part of the American public debate. The argument should never have been about whether evangelicals ought to be involved in worldly issues, but rather about which matters they should be most concerned and the most prudent ways to express such convictions. It is the duty of Christians to be concerned citizens, to indeed strive, as Richard John Neuhaus has said, "to build a world in which the strong are just, and power is tempered by mercy, in which the weak are nurtured and the marginal embraced, and those at the entrance gates and those at the exit gates of life are protected both by law and love."

Working for economic, political, and social change often requires the patience of Job, because politics is, as Max Weber once said, "the slow boring of hard surfaces." Many evangelicals have learned that politics frequently requires prudent and principled compromise, that it is the art of the possible and not the reign of the saints. Some have even learned through the hard knocks of battles fought, victories won, and disappointments beyond measure, that politics is, because of the effects of the original Fall of Man, "the art of finding approximate solutions to basically insoluble problems," as Reinhold Niebuhr so aptly put it.

Evangelicals of every perspective no longer need to be convinced that economic, political, and social concerns are an important part of Christian discipleship. It is a settled issue that "the least of these" among us is to be treated with both charity *and* justice. The debates center now around prudential questions regarding which politics are in fact the most effective in meeting the normative standards of justice. Many times these are empirical questions that need honest exploration and evaluation.

So, despite the demise of the Moral Majority, despite the disappointments for those who supported the Pat Robertson campaign for president in 1988, despite the waning influence of radical evangelicals, and even despite disillusionment with aspects of the Reagan and Bush presidencies (whether the critique is from the left or the right), and despite the election of Bill Clinton, many evangelicals are as resolute as ever. While the problems of the modern world will not soon disappear, it is the existence of those very problems that will keep evangelicals engaged in economic, social, political, and cultural activism. Evangelicals and fundamentalists are quick to remind us that this age, like all ages, is "standing in the need of prayer." The ravages brought on our culture by economic, political, and social injustice, by secularization, and by modernity are formidable, but, as evangelicals have always insisted, miracles still happen and grace has always been amazing. And for the love of Christ and the duties of charity entailed by following Him, they will continue to be engaged, not only with the world, but, because of their own diversity, with each other.

Compassionate Capitalism

Dick DeVos

Dick DeVos is president of Amway Corporation, one of the world's largest direct selling corporations. Additionally, he is founder and chairman of the board of Windquest Groups, a privately held management concern that owns and operates multiple companies in the manufacturing, financial, and international trading sectors, and he is president of the Orlando Magic NBA basketball team. Prior to becoming president of Amway, he worked at the company for 15 years in a variety of positions, including vice president of its international division. Under his leadership, Amway's international sales tripled and they exceeded domestic sales for the first time in the history of the company.

Mr. DeVos has also served on a variety of boards and commissions, including the Michigan Jobs Commission, the Michigan Association of Non-Public Schools, the White House Commission on Presidential Scholars, the United Negro College Fund Drive, the Republican Congressional Leadership Council, the Federalist Society, the Grand Rapids YMCA, and the LaGrave Christian Reformed Church.

The great car maker Henry Ford was once asked to contribute to a new hospital. The billionaire pledged $5,000. But the next day a newspaper headline read: "Henry Ford contributes *$50,000* to local hospital." Ford immediately complained to the fundraiser that he had been misunderstood. So the fundraiser said he would ask the newspaper to print a retraction to read: "Henry Ford reduces his donation by $45,000." Of course, Ford realized the potential for negative publicity, and he knew he was stuck with giving the larger amount. He agreed to give the $50,000 with one stipulation. Above the entrance to the hospital was to be carved the biblical inscription, "I came among you, and you took me in."

Here's the paradox: Did having to be coerced into a larger donation make Henry Ford a miser and an immoral member of the marketplace? Or did the fact that his success gave him the ability to help build a hospital make the marketplace moral?

The Principles of Business as Effective Tools

Like any other segment of society, the marketplace is only as moral or immoral as its members. But the principles of business can be effective tools in the hands of the moral entrepreneur. While not perfect, the marketplace is one of the best places today for the moral entrepreneur to serve society and inspire others to do good.

In thinking about the theme of this volume, I wondered, why morality and the *marketplace?* Why not morality and politics ... or morality and the media ... or the church? After all, we have all seen the headlines about moral issues in each of those institutions. Yet morality in the *marketplace* is most often the focus for discussion because the marketplace is the most suspect. The public image of business as immoral and unethical has persisted throughout history.

The competitive nature of business and survival through achievement leads to a climate in which different people will use different methods in their attempts to flourish. Whether it is sports or school, or any other endeavor that tests our abilities, some play by the rules, and some do not. We all have seen this from our earliest days in the classroom and our childhood games on the playground.

Testing Our Moral Values

There's the story of the English professor who is suspicious of a superior work turned in by one of her below-average students. She asked the student, "Did you write this poem without any outside help?" The student told her that he did indeed write the poem on his own. And she responded, "That's amazing. To think that I am honored to have in *my* class—Lord Byron."

Whether it is in school, in business, or on the playing field, competition and the desire to succeed test our moral values. Some pass the test. And some fail. That is because life is largely a do-it-yourself (with help from above) project. It does not *take* all kinds—we just *have* all kinds. As a *National Geographic* photographer replied when asked about his career, "There are a million ways to get from birth to death—and they all work."

NBA coach Pat Riley often talks about temptations in basketball. He says each player must have a strong code of ethics in order to resist the temptations of large incomes, inflated egos, and the easy opportunities players have for immoral conduct. Riley says his players have to be especially careful because crossing the line is so easy. They have to realize, as a wise man once observed, that the ten commandments are *not* the ten suggestions. In basketball or business, we need a solid moral foundation in order to resist the snares of increasing abundance and opportunity.

My father, Rich DeVos, has heard all the critics who label business as opportunistic and Amway as materialistic. He named his latest book *Compassionate Capitalism* because the title appears to many as a contradiction in terms. How can capitalism be compassionate? Capitalism *is* compassionate—when it is in the hands of *compassionate people*. The marketplace is not inherently immoral. But its temptations can breed immorality in the business person who enters the marketplace without a set of redeeming values.

No Charity Without Profit

As the Bible tells us, "It is easier for a camel to pass through the eye of a needle than for a rich man to enter the kingdom of heaven." In today's business vernacular, we would call that a slippery slope. It should give pause to anyone contemplating striking it rich. The wisdom of the Bible recognizes that with greater wealth comes greater temptations. We all know that power can corrupt. Money can fuel greed. We can be possessed by our possessions. And personal gain can make us forget the better part of our nature and forget the needs of others.

These traits are what inspired one of the most famous characters in literature. In *A Christmas Carol,* Charles Dickens revealed how Ebenezer Scrooge gained the world and lost his soul. Scrooge was a successful businessman. But his love of riches replaced his love for others. He isolated himself from friends and family, mistreated his employees, and ignored the needs of his community. His spirit could not even be revived once a year at Christmas.

But that was not the end of the story. As you recall, Scrooge *did* change. And the way Scrooge promised to "keep Christmas in his heart every day" makes another interesting point about morality in the marketplace. Remember what Scrooge did to mend his ways? On the Christmas morning of his transformation, the first thing he did was to give a poor boy a handsome reward to run an errand. He bought food and gifts for his employee Bob Cratchit's family. He gave Cratchit a huge raise and promised a job to Cratchit's son. He gave Cratchit more holiday time off to spend with his family. He provided the funds needed for an operation to save Tiny Tim's life. And he gave generously to the poor. Everything Scrooge did to help others was possible because of his success in business.

Some suggest, of course, that the lesson of Scrooge is that money is the root of all evil. But the Bible says it is the *love* of money. It is not a sin to be successful. Only the fortunate can help the less fortunate. Thus, Scrooge in reality provides this lesson: There can be no charity without profit, and the more profit there is, the more potential for charity.

Economic Vices and Virtues

Economic vices and virtues do not fall into simple categories. Consider, for example, envy, pride, and greed. I think most of us would agree these are potential vices in the marketplace. But they are part of our human nature, and as such they also are raw materials that can be refined into higher ideals in the marketplace—ideals that serve the best interest of customers, employ people, and enhance the quality of life for all. Pride can be a vice. But pride of workmanship produces quality and innovation. Greed is not good, but a desire for material gain can become the motivation to succeed in a business that provides jobs for thousands. Envy is not a desirable trait. But it can spark the spirit of competition that results in the production of better products and the development of human potential.

Consider some of the principles of free enterprise that support morality—not only in the marketplace, but in society as a whole:

—*Businesses must serve the needs and wants of customers to be successful.* To survive and compete, a company must make the best product at the best price, which ensures fair treatment of customers. The creator of the Hershey Chocolate Bar was once asked how his product could become so popular without the use of advertising. Milton Hershey said, "Give them quality. That's the best kind of advertising."

—*The wealth and innovation created by business improves the quality of life for all men.* Through advances in science and technology made practical by business, we live longer and more comfortably, earn higher incomes, have an abundance of products, require less labor, and have more leisure.

—*Businesses provide the best benefits to attract the best employees.* This makes the marketplace a major health care provider and source of other benefits. And it inspires people to be their best in order to land the best jobs. It is considered a signal honor in business circles to be included in the book, *The 100 Best Companies to Work for in America.*

—*Business is a major supporter of cultural and charitable causes.* In Grand Rapids, we annually raise millions of dollars for United Way. The campaign is possible because of the volunteer work of business people and the dollars donated by companies and their employees. Amway, for example, is a major contributor to the Easter Seal Society. Last year our contribution was *$2.1 million.* And it was mostly raised by our independent distributors—people who wanted to share their success with others.

In Grand Rapids, we are also proud to point to our performing arts centers, museums, college buildings, and other public institutions. Much of our skyline and our general quality of life is the result of successful business people who wanted to give something back to their community. In our city and across the country, our public institutions bear the names of the entrepreneurs who donate money and lead the fundraising campaigns to build them.

—*Business is a good neighbor.* To enhance community relations and build their image, most companies sponsor projects that ultimately benefit the public. Amway is a partner with an inner-city Grand Rapids school in an effort to enhance the education of underprivileged children. Worldwide, we support projects such as "Clean-up Australia," art programs for children in Germany and Hong Kong, and tours in Japan by the San Francisco Symphony and other renowned orchestras. And these are just a few of many sponsorships by one company.

I could list hundreds of examples of how the private sector and the free market require fair play, cooperative team work, development of talents, charity, and high moral standards. But the few I have listed are sufficient to make a good case against those who see an inherent evil in people who choose to succeed in business. In fact, success in business is one of the best opportunities we have today for building values and creating an atmosphere where the moral person can flourish.

Sir John Marks Templeton, the prominent financier and investment advisor, said this about applying the gospel within the free market system: "The Parable of the Talents tells us we should use to the utmost whatever talents the Lord has given to us. This is entrepreneurship. Entrepreneurs find better and better ways to produce and to serve."

Compassionate Capitalism is subtitled, *People Helping People to Help Themselves.* Rich DeVos says that is the heart of the Amway business. Growing up in Amway, I have met thousands of distributors who believe that you do not get ahead by leaving your values behind. Many of them have fine homes, cars, boats, and every other material possession that people associate with success. The dream of material wealth may have been their original motivation. But if you ask them now about what it means to be successful, few mention possessions. They focus on the intrinsic values of success. They talk about their satisfaction in developing their talents to their full potential and their satisfaction in helping others do the same. They cite the extra time success has given them to spend with their families or to volunteer within their communities. They communicate the joy of sharing their success with others.

In *Against the Night*, Charles Colson includes a chapter called "Men Without Chests." It is based on an observation by C.S. Lewis. Lewis says that the chest is the center of our spirit. Our head is the center of our rational thought. And our stomach is the home of our appetites. The chest keeps our head and stomach in check. When we live only by our appetites and logic, notes Lewis, we deny our spirit and become "men without chests." Colson adds, "This might well describe today's inside traders, corrupt politicians, and pulpiteers."

Colson goes on: "Societies are tragically vulnerable when the men and women who compose them lack character. A nation or culture cannot long endure unless it is undergirded by common values such as valor, public-spirit, and respect for others and the law. It cannot stand unless it is populated by people who will act on motives superior to their own immediate interest." That is also what is required for morality in the marketplace. And I can tell you from my years in business that most of the entrepreneurs I meet are not "men without chests."

The Power of the Entrepreneur to Serve

Consider for a moment a common household and business tool we all use everyday. Think of the telephone. Whether it is on my desk at the office, in my car, or at home, I know I could not live without a telephone—even though at times I think I would like to try. But I think we all can agree the telephone is essential.

Much of the wealth created by today's global market-place would not be possible without the telephone and the telephone lines that send information immediately around the world. Beyond business, the telephone's 911 emergency system saves thousands of lives and helps protect homes and property. And as telephone companies like to remind us, telephones keep families and friends in touch.

The inventor of the telephone, Alexander Graham Bell, could never have dreamed how his invention would change the world. Living in the 19th century, he never set out to invent something for our commerce and convenience in the 20th century. His mother was deaf, and he married a deaf woman. The telephone was a by-product of his lifelong passion to invent a device that could help the deaf hear. He spent part of his life teaching in schools for the deaf. Had he settled for that calling, he would have led an admirable life. But he would have served only a small community in need and been forgotten. As an inventor and compassionate entrepreneur, his work continues to have a profound impact on each one of us. Bell is one of a multitude of examples of the power of the entrepreneur to serve.

There is another story that makes this same point in a different way. It is about the son of a struggling peddler. From his father, this boy learned how to earn and keep money. From his mother, he learned to put God first in his life, to be honest, and to help others. Later on he said, "From the beginning, I was trained to work, to save, and to give." In his first job as a bookkeeper earning 50 cents a day, he tithed from his first paycheck. He gave to his church, a foreign mission, and the poor.

In 1865 he joined a fellow church member in the growing industry of oil refining. He concentrated on producing a quality product by plowing his profits back into the business. He produced kerosene so cheaply that it became the most efficient source for lighting American homes, streets, and factories. For the first time in history, working class people could afford to light their homes at night. By 1870 working and reading after dark became new activities for most Americans.

The young industrialist continued his philosophy of cutting costs. He purchased the inefficient operations of his competitors and undercut the prices of his foreign competition. During the 1870s the price of kerosene dropped from 26 cents to 8 cents a gallon. And he captured about 90 percent of the American market. He went on to own one of the largest oil companies in the world. Yet the more money he made, the more he gave away. By the time he died, he had given away $550 million—more than any other American before him had ever *possessed.*

Beyond that, his production of affordable fuels for lighting and for powering cars enhanced every American's quality of life. As I am sure you have guessed by now, he was John D. Rockefeller, founder of Standard Oil. I refrained from mentioning his name until the end of the story because I didn't want to prejudice your opinion. Unfortunately, the Rockefeller name conjures up more negative than positive connotations in the minds of many. Another contributor to this volume, Burton W. Folsom, Jr., has done an excellent job of defending Rockefeller and other entrepreneurs in his book, *The Myth of the Robber Barons,* but still, stereotypes die hard.

Despite the evils so often associated with money and profit—greed, pride, envy, power—the marketplace *is* also the place where good and virtue thrive, where cooperation, charity, and compassion make their full force felt in our lives.

The responsiblity for morality in the marketplace rests with all of us. As customers, the marketplace is our servant, and, as entrepreneurs, it is our tool. As customers, we are responsible for demanding that the marketplace serves our best interests, and, as entrepreneurs, we are responsible for demanding that it serves much more.

Recovering the Original American Vision

Peter Marshall

A Presbyterian minister who has gained national recognition as an evangelist and teacher, Rev. Peter Marshall conducts evangelistic crusades and preaching missions in cities across the country and appears in a number of Christian education video and audio series. Ordained in 1965, he served 12 years in pastoral ministry before devoting himself to national ministry and writing. He is the coauthor with David Manuel of two best-selling children's books, *The Light and the Glory* (Baker Book House, 1992) and *From Sea to Shining Sea* (Baker Book House, 1993). A third book, *Mine Eyes Have Seen the Glory,* is now in preparation.

Rev. Marshall's vocation has family origins: He is the son of Dr. Peter Marshall, the former chaplain of the U.S. Senate, and Catherine Marshall LeSourd, author of such best-selling books as *Christy* (currently also a network television series) and *A Man Called Peter,* which was made into one of 20th Century Fox's most successful films ever and tells the story of how Rev. Marshall's father, a young Scottish immigrant, became one of America's greatest preachers.

America began as a religious nation. John Adams, the second president of the United States, wrote, "Our Constitution was designed only for a moral and religious people. It is wholly inadequate for the government of any other." What Adams was saying, in other words, was that if we fail to practice basic values like honesty, charity, and piety the Constitution itself will cease to function, and American society will fall apart.

Another famous Adams—Samuel Adams—said, "When once the people lose their virtue, they will be ready to surrender their liberties to the first external or internal invader."

Portions of this chapter have appeared in *The Light and the Glory* by Peter Marshall and David Manuel (Fleming Revell, 1977).

Virtue was "their great security." And James Madison, the chief architect of our Constitution and fourth president of the United States, said, "We have staked the whole of our political institutions on the capacity of mankind to govern itself ... according to the commandments of God."

In our secular age it comes as a shock to many modern Americans to realize that the founding fathers thought like that. But to these men America was nothing less than a divine experiment in self-government, the only one in world history. It was a nation deliberately founded on Biblical principles of self-government. It was also founded on capitalist principles, since men not only had to be free to make their own way in the world but to freely choose all their own actions, including those in the marketplace.

But for decades we have been taught that capitalism in America was really an oppressive system of economics founded on greed. Nothing could be further from the truth. The only way in which an entrepreneur can develop new ideas or start a new business venture is to practice the opposite of greed: self-sacrifice. He must plow his profits back into his business. He must work hard, investing time as well as money. He must discipline himself. Greed is the very essence of self-indulgence, but true entrepreneurship and the development of new ideas and new business enterprises are the essence of self-discipline.

American capitalism is also clearly based on the Protestant work ethic, as well as on the idea that in order to succeed one must produce something that will be a blessing in other people's lives. Capitalism is attacked as immoral by people who know little about their nation's roots, which are firmly grounded in the Judeo-Christian tradition *and* free enterprise. We must spread the truth about those roots if we are to recover our basic values; we must recover the vision of America upon which our nation was founded.

President Woodrow Wilson once forcefully declared: "A nation which does not remember what it was yesterday, does not know what it is today, nor what it is trying to do." He continued, "We are trying to do a futile thing if we do not

know where we came from or what we have been about."
Exactly right. Even Karl Marx, the father of communism,
agreed: "Take away the heritage of a people, and they are
easily persuaded." If we don't know our roots and where we
came from and who we are, we can fall for anything.

That is what has been happening to Americans for most
of this century. Our history, literature, and economics texts
have been rewritten by "revisionists." Because of the intellectual cynicism that prevailed on both sides of the Atlantic after
the horrible slaughter of World War I, mottoes like West
Point's "Duty, Honor, and Country" fell very much out of
fashion. And starting in the 1920s, hundreds of new books
were written solely in order to disprove common "myths"
about the founding of America. The Christian faith of our
forefathers, and that faith's relationship to capitalism, were,
of course, ruthlessly censored in the process.

The seriousness of losing our heritage is revealed by a
Scripture verse, Judges 2:10, which says, "And all that generation also were gathered to their fathers, and there arose
another generation after them who did not know the Lord
or the works He had done for Israel." That is us. We have
no idea these days what God has done in our own American
past.

The Old Testament tells us that Nehemiah was the cup-
bearer to the king of Persia. God brought him back from
exile to preside over the physical rebuilding of the walls
around the Holy City of Jerusalem. I believe we are the
Nehemiahs of today. God is telling us to rebuild the moral
and spiritual walls of our society. But how do we know what
to do? We have to discover His plan. Another Scripture
verse, Psalm 44:1, says, "We have heard with our ears, God,
our fathers have told us, what wondrous deeds thou didst in
their days, the days of old." The problem in America is that
we stopped listening to our forefathers generations ago. Let
us look at just one episode early on in our history to discover
what our forefathers have to tell us.

Massachusetts Bay: A Failing Company

On June 8, 1630, John Winthrop stood at the rail of the
Arbella, and got his first sight of New England: the fir-cov-
ered hills of Maine. He stared in wonder at pines taller than
any tree he had ever seen coming right down to the boulders
on the shore. The afternoon sun was shining and an irides-
cent haze hung over the hills so that the firs seemed to glis-
ten. . . .

It was so much grander than he had somehow expected.
Breathtakingly beautiful, but wild and savage, too. This was
not a land to be cleared and settled easily. His heart welled
within him, as it occurred to him that even this forbidding
wildness was a blessing, for it would discourage any who
came for selfish reasons. A fresh, clear breeze came out to
them over the sun-dappled waters, bearing the scent of those
majestic pines, "and there came a smell off the shore like the
smell of a garden."[1]

A peaceful passage may not seem particularly notewor-
thy, but in those days it was considered another manifestation of God's special grace. As Edward Johnson, an amateur
historian and contemporary of Winthrop, put it in the opening words of his *Wonder-Working Providences of Sion's Saviour
in New England,* "Then judge, all you (whom the Lord hath
given a discerning spirit), whether these poor New England
people be not forerunners of Christ's army, and the marvelous providences which you shall now hear, be not the very
finger of God." And in his first example, in this highly enthusiastic compendium of instances of divine intervention, he
pointed out that, at a time when so many ships were going
down in storms or being taken by pirates and privateers, only
one of the 1987 vessels to set sail for New England in the first
half of the seventeenth century was ever lost!

On the morning of June 1, they came upon a cheerful
sight: a ship at anchor with half a dozen fishing shallops
around her, all bobbing up and down. A little while later, the
captain informed Winthrop that they had Cape Ann in sight,
which meant that they would be making Salem Harbor on

next morning's tide. Salem at last! After seventy-two days of waiting!

But the sight which greeted them the following morning was far from cheerful. Where was Salem? Surely this pitiful collection of huts and hovels and canvas shelters—surely this was not the first town of the Massachusetts Bay Company? It must be just the remnants of their first camp, temporary housing which they had not bothered to dismantle. That was it; the main town must be further in the woods.

But as the ship drew nearer, the truth sank in: This *was* Salem. And then the people came down to the shore—gaunt and ragged-looking, glad to see the new arrivals, but something was wrong. It was something more important than their thinness or the sorry condition of their clothing—something inside of them.... They were listless, slow of movement, apathetic. The life was gone out of their faces, their expressions.

Deeply troubled, Winthrop went ashore in the first boat, and was met by John Endecott, the brash, quick-tempered soldier who had acted as governor for the now-defunct New England Company, and was filling in as provisional governor for the Massachusetts Bay Company. As soon as was politic, Winthrop arranged for a private briefing with the man he would replace. From Endecott, he learned that of the sixty-six men who had come over with him in 1628, and the two hundred who accompanied Higginson and Skelton the following year, scarcely eighty-five remained. More than eighty had died, while the rest had quit and gone back to England. And many of those who were left were intending to do the same.

It is not difficult to imagine the sort of exchange that probably followed: "But my good heavens, man, what's to become of the plantation? This is as bad as Jamestown!" Winthrop might have exclaimed, "and these people aren't fortune hunters; they're decent puritans! You had ministers here, good ones! Is there no teaching here?"

"We have a teaching service on Thursdays," Endecott would have hotly defended himself," and two services on Sundays!" He sighed. "But it seems to do no good. They hear the words and nod, and nothing changes." And his voice trailed off in the same defeat which Winthrop had noted outside.

Winthrop spent that night aboard the *Arbella,* undoubtedly availing himself of the privacy of the captain's cabin. It began to look as if the final curtain would ring down before the play could finish the first act. He had not even had a chance to put into practice some of the insights he felt the Lord had given him on the long voyage over. Was it all for nothing? Had he not heard God, after all? Had his selfishness or pride put all their lives into jeopardy?

He may have walked over to the port then, and looked out, recalling another time he had stood at that same port. . . .

A City upon a Hill

Outside, a green-white wake trailed erratically behind them on the surface of the ocean, as they yawed this way and that under a lead-gray sky. He had been thinking for a long time about the plantation, and the quality of life which they could have together. Now, in a rush of inspiration, it was all coming together in his mind. Like all men trained to work in written words, he yearned to get out his writing box, and ink and paper, but he restrained himself until the concepts were clearly formed.

The sea had moderated somewhat, when he finally went to the chart table and took out the box. Selecting a quill, he sharpened it, dipped it into the wide-bottomed ink bottle, carefully removing the excess against the rim, and looked at the white sheet of paper before him.

What he would write next would rank in importance with the compact which the pilgrims had drawn up aboard the *Mayflower.* Indeed, he took their concept one step further. For while they had stated what they were about to do as a body politic of equal members, gathered under God, and to be governed by their mutual consent, Winthrop now spelled out why it would work. His definition of covenant love has seldom been equaled.

A MODEL OF CHRISTIAN CHARITY were the words that went across the top of the sheet of paper. He went straight to the heart of the matter, beginning with some thoughts on the nature of man's love for his neighbor—what it could and should be, by the grace of God.

> This love among Christians is a real thing, not imaginary.... As absolutely necessary to the [well] being of the Body of Christ, as the sinews and other ligaments of a natural body are to the [well] being of that body ... We are a company, professing ourselves fellow members of Christ, [and thus] we ought to account ourselves knit together by this bond of love....

Then came the heart of his vision:

> Thus stands the cause between God and us: We are entered into covenant with Him for this work. We have taken out a Commission; the Lord hath given us leave to draw our own articles.... If the Lord shall please to hear us, and bring us in peace to the place we desire, then hath He ratified this Covenant and sealed our Commission, [and] will expect a strict performance of the Articles contained in it. But if we shall neglect the observance of these Articles ... the Lord will surely break out in wrath against us.
>
> Now the only way to avoid this shipwreck and to provide for our posterity, is to follow the counsel of Micah, to do justly, to love mercy, to walk humbly with our God. For this end, we must be knit together in this work as one man.... We must hold a familiar commerce together in all meekness, gentleness, patience, and liberality. We must delight in each other, make one another's condition our own, rejoice together, mourn together, labor and suffer together, always having before our eyes our Commission and Community in this work, as members of the same body. So shall we keep the unity of the Spirit in the bond of peace....
>
> We shall find that the God of Israel is among us, when ten of us shall be able to resist a thousand of our enemies, when He shall make us a praise and glory, that men of succeeding plantations shall say, "The Lord make it like that of New England." For we must consider that we shall be as a City upon a Hill....[2]

Standing now at the port and looking out at the New England night, Winthrop knew that it was God who had brought that previous time to mind, as if to remind him that He would not have given him this momentous revelation, had He not intended it to be put to use.

Winthrop soon learned what had happened that winter of 1628–1629. They had suffered a general sickness of the same sort that had stricken Plymouth during its first winter. In fact, Endecott had written Governor Bradford, appealing for help. Bradford's response was to send their doctor, Samuel Fuller, who had by now had abundant experience in treating cases of scurvy and constitutions gravely weakened by long sea voyages, as well as the various fevers and illnesses accompanying a sharp, cold winter.

Fuller stayed through the winter in Endecott's house and helped substantially. Indeed, Endecott was so impressed that he named their settlement *Salem*, the Hebrew word for peace. For this Separatist whom he had been prepared to dislike had manifested more Christian love than any Puritan he knew. The two men had often talked late by the fire. And the more Endecott learned, the more respectful he became of what God was doing forty miles down the coast.

The Success of Plymouth

Doctor Fuller was also a deacon, and Endecott was especially interested in the structure of their church. The Plymouth church, under the leadership of Elder Brewster, was organizationally separate from the civil authority under Governor Bradford. Yet it obviously exercised decisive moral influence over it. Separatist church leadership was provided by a pastor, a teacher, and a ruling elder, but these were chosen by the membership of the church (*not* imposed by a presbytery or hierarchy of Bishops). The right to choose freely their own spiritual leadership was zealously guarded as one of the basic tenets of their Christian faith. What was more, the Separatist church was open to all who cared to worship there. But to become a *member* of the church (and thus to be eligible to vote in both civil and religious elections), one had to convince the eldership of the church of one's personal, saving relationship with Jesus Christ, and of the orthodoxy of one's faith.

Winthrop may have had some private doubts about the wisdom of giving the right to vote to non-landholders (the idea of servants having equal voting rights with their masters smacked of "democracy"), but he held his tongue. Whatever Plymouth was doing, from all reports God was blessing them more abundantly each successive year. And there was no question of the fact that regardless of how radical their system, Plymouth was primarily interested in seeking and doing God's will. According to Endecott, Bradford declared the day before their annual election to be a day of prayer: People were not to work, but to pray for the Lord's will, as to whom He wanted them to vote into office. Under those conditions, even democractic government might work!

The more Endecott had listened to Dr. Fuller, the more convinced he had become that this was the church model which God intended Salem to follow as well. Thus, when the Reverends Higginson and Skelton had arrived, he told them of his decision. They insisted that they were loyal to the Church of England, but since they themselves had not settled on any particular church structure before coming, they were open and receptive to Endecott's proposals. (When one considers the combinations of timing and circumstance which produced the Congregational Church, one is left in awe of God's handiwork). So they were duly elected pastor and teacher, though their formal installation would have to wait until the arrival of whomever the partners elected as governor.

Of the "gathering" of this first Puritan church in America, we have a vivid contemporary account from the pen of the enthusiastic reporter Edward Johnson:

> Although the number of the faithful people of Christ were but few, yet their longing to gather into a church was very great.... Having fasted and prayed with humble acknowledgment of their own unworthiness to be called of Christ to so worthy a work, they joined together in a holy Covenant with the Lord and with one another, promising by the Lord's

assistance to walk together in exhorting, admonishing and rebuking one another, and to cleave to the Lord with a full purpose of heart. . . .[3]

As Endecott was relating the account of their covenanting with God and one another, Winthrop may very well have interrupted him. "Then that is why it's not working!" he might have exclaimed.

Endecott stared at him. "I don't understand."

"Don't you see? They love God, and they've covenanted to obey Him, or they wouldn't be here. But they're not living out their covenant with one another. They don't love one another enough to exhort, admonish, and rebuke. And at Plymouth they do. That's the difference!"

"But," Endecott objected, "the Separatists at Plymouth— or the First Comers, as we call them—already had been a church for years before they came, and we've only just gathered here."

"All the more reason why we've got to live up to our covenant with each other!" Winthrop paused and looked straight at Endecott. "And it must begin with the leadership. Unless you and I demonstrate our own commitment to this plantation and to these people, unless you and I are willing to put *our* whole lives into the work here, we can't expect *them* to. Well?"

Endecott met his gaze. "You can count on it," he said.

"Good. Now, first of all, I want to get settled ashore right away. This house is large enough to accommodate both of us, is it not?"

"But Mr. Winthrop, this is *your* house; it goes to whomever is Governor. I'll find lodgings elsewhere."

"If you had room for Dr. Fuller over the winter, there is room for both of us, until we newcomers can build a place of our own."

Before Endecott could reply, he went onto the next thing on his mind. "An hour before noon, have every able-bodied man and boy assembled in the center of town." He thought for a moment. "And have the women come, too, those that are healthy and are not needed to tend the sick."

He glanced at the height of the sun. "In the meantime, I will see about getting my belongings ashore and stored here."

Winthrop started out the door, then turned back. "Oh, and tell the gentlemen—Mr. Saltonstall, Mr. Pynchon, Mr. Nowell, and the others—that this includes them, too." And he smiled, "You'd better suggest that they wear old clothes,"

"Right, Mr. Winthrop," Endecott said, and nodded.

Promptly at one o'clock, he came to the opening in the center of the huts and shelters that was "town." A number of people were already there, staring at their governor in amazement. Dressed in worn boots and breeches and an old frayed shirt, he looked more like an indentured servant than a gentleman.

When most of the people had gathered, he addressed them: "The situation here is not exactly what we in England were led to expect." There was some cynical laughter, but mostly silence; they were waiting to hear what would come next. "But I think it can be rectified without too much trouble, although it's going to require hard work. By the end of the summer, every one of you is going to be in a proper dwelling. Until then, more than one family will have to live together, at least for the first winter." There was now a noticeable current of unbelief. "How are we going to do it?" Winthrop asked for them, "By God's grace, we are going to do it, and by helping one another,"

Laborers in God's Vineyard

At that moment, he was interrupted by Richard Saltonstall and a friend, who were just then arriving and carrying on a conversation of their own. Saltonstall was wearing a white shirt with a ruff at the neck. Winthrop's lips compressed, then he turned back to the rest.

"First of all, who among you has had any experience fishing?"

Eight men raised their hands, and Winthrop conferred with Endecott at his side. "All right, Packham and Kenworthy, each of you take three men, and on alternate days you will take turns using the shallop for fishing.

"Now, the women," he said, looking up from his lists. "Those of you who are able, will do field work in the mornings. The rest will be under Mr. Skelton on nursing detail. Mr. Skelton, as of this moment, you are officially responsible for what you and Mr. Higginson have been unofficially doing all along: tending the sick. Only now you are going to have more help.

"Mr. Higginson," and here he turned to the pastor who had lowered himself to a stump because he was unable to stand any longer, "considering your condition, sir, you can help us most with your prayers—and a strong word on Sunday about what it means to serve God and one another."

He returned his attention to the other minister. "Mr. Skelton, you will also be in charge of the food stores. I want an inventory taken daily, and I would appreciate your alerting me of any projected shortfalls, as far in advance as possible. Also, by the guidance of the Holy Spirit, you are to decide what the daily ration will be. And those of you who have your own stocks will be expected to forego your ration."

He folded the lists and handed them to Endecott. "The rest of you will form into two work parties: those under forty, with Mr. Endecott, those over forty, with me. Are there any questions?"

"Yes." It was Richard Saltonstall. "John, you do not really expect *me* to—"

"Yes, Richard, I really do."

"But common labor, John! I brought nine men with me to look after that sort of thing! And you brought more than I!"

Winthrop hesitated before replying. "Last August, at Cambridge, you put your name to an agreement which bound you as a Christian to be ready in your person to further this work. So did I. This work will not succeed unless every man is willing to give his all. We are all laborers in God's vineyard, and that does not mean that, just because we can afford to, we pay someone else to do our work for us."

Saltonstall shook his head, almost too angry to speak. "This is—"

"This is the way it is going to be, I'm afraid. And I will tell you something else," he looked around. "This is for all of you who were late. I want you to know that I do not consider lateness to be merely impolite; as far as I am concerned, it is a sin against God! This is His work, and He has called us to it. To steal His time is to blaspheme against what He is trying to accomplish here!

"Starting tomorrow morning, we will meet here promptly at two hours past sunrise for daily work assignments. And bring something with you to eat at the noon hour. We will work until four hours past noon, and the rest of the day is entirely your own." There was more laughter now.

"Are there any other questions?" There were none.

Without doubt, a miracle took place upon Winthrop's arrival: A nearly dead colony was resurrected. And from all reports, God's single instrument in this resurrection was John Winthrop. Cotton Mather would refer to Winthrop as *Nehemias Americanus* in reference to the Old Testament leader I mentioned earlier who had brought the Israelites back from their Babylonian exile to the Promised Land and who directed the rebuilding of the walls of Jerusalem.[4] But more important, Winthrop, like Nehemiah, had inspired them to resume their covenant with God.

Another seventeenth-century report, quoted by modern Yale historian Edmund Morgan in his biography of Winthrop, said: "[So soon] as Mr. Winthrop was landed, perceiving what misery was like to ensue through their idleness, he presently fell to work with his own hands, and thereby so encouraged the rest that there was not an idle person then to be found in the whole plantation. And whereas the Indians said they [the newcomers] would shortly return as fast as they came, now they admired to see in what short time they had housed themselves and planted corn sufficient for their subsistence."[5]

To be sure, they endured the same general sickness which seemed to afflict every shipload of settlers. And a few days after their arrival, Winthrop suffered the grievous loss of his son, Henry, who was drowned in a fishing accident.

But the tragedy seemed to redouble his dedication to the business of planting the colony (much as a similar tragedy had affected William Bradford before him).

It was a sustained enthusiasm. Three months after his arrival, as he was about to lead the bulk of the newcomers to their final settling place in Boston (for there were now more than a thousand, far too many for Salem to absorb), he wrote his wife Margaret, "I thank God, I like so well to be here.. And if I were to come again, I would not have altered my course, though I had foreseen all these afflictions. I never fared better in my life, never slept better, never had more contentedness of mind."[6]

The Kingdom of God in America

The example of the Massachusetts Bay colony teaches us some vital lessons about our roots and about the theme of this volume, which is morality and the marketplace.

The first lesson is that, despite what the revisionists claim, our forefathers came to America in order to build a society based on obedience to God. They wanted their religion to govern every aspect of their lives, including their economy.

The second lesson is that our forefathers believed in freedom, but not freedom to do whatever they pleased—freedom to do what God pleased. This was reflected in their political system, which, although a far cry from modern republican government, was an important advance for individual liberty.

The third lesson is that our forefathers believed that it was not only necessary to succeed in the marketplace but to reap the benefits of economic success. During the emergency that immediately confronted Winthrop's group, everyone had to work; there were no handouts. Once the emergency was over, individuals were free to pursue their own businesses, and they rapidly made the colonization of New England a smashing commercial as well as a spiritual success. They did not view this success as the result of self-interest but of obedience to their covenant with God and with one another. Their views on the sanctity of the covenant directly informed their view of contracts, which, along with their view on personal virtue, is the foundation of all economic activity.

Most important, the Massachusetts Bay Company reminds us of the need to work together. Jesus told his disciples, "A house divided against itself shall not stand," (Matthew 12:25) and with each New England church community, God was building a house, not just assembling a pile of stones. As Peter wrote to new Christians, "Come and as living stones be yourselves built into a spiritual house" (1 Peter 2:5) In the rocky fields of New England, God was raising a kingdom of stone houses, with each stone in each house fitted into place by Him. This kingdom would be as close as a family, a spiritual family which would be able to withstand the most implacable pressure the world could bring to bear. As we were coming to see, these stone houses were in turn to be the foundation stones, not merely of American republicanism, or American free enterprise—two wonderful and interconnected blessings for which we should be eternally grateful—but of this divine experiment that we call America.

Notes

1. Edward Johnson, *The Wonder-Working Providences of Sion's Saviour in New England,* 1653, J. Frankin Jameson, editor (Barnes and Noble, 1910), 61.

2. *The Winthrop Papers,* II (Boston Historical Society), 92–295.

3. Johnson, 46–47.

4. Cotton Mather, *Magnalia Christi Americana,* Book II, as quoted in Sacvan Bercovitch, *The Puritan Origins of the American Self* (New Haven: Yale University Press, 1975), 1.

5. Edmund S. Morgan, *The Puritan Dilemma* (Boston: Little, Brown & Co., 1958), 58.

6. *Winthrop Papers,* 313.

Reading 1: The Powerful and the Powerless

Jim Wallis

In Jim Wallis's view, "a totalitarian spirit fuels the engines of both Wall Street and the Kremlin." Wallis says that America's pursuit of "self-interested empire-building" causes much of the poverty and revolutionary violence throughout the world. A prominent leader of "radical evangelicals," Wallis believes that the U.S. government only pretends to support freedom movements while actually engaging in an "expansionist thrust" in foreign affairs. He writes that "the uncritical acceptance of the myth of 'the national interest' and 'national security' is essential in keeping the United States the number one nation."

Calling for redistribution of the world's wealth and political power, he argues that people in the undeveloped countries of the world are poor because residents of the United States are rich. Furthermore, the poverty of the poor is maintained by the economic and political systems of the United States.

He chides evangelical churches for practicing "compassionless inactivity," and declares that Americans' "over-consumption is theft from the poor." He summons Christians to be "radically obedient" to the Gospel of Christ: "If our lives are secure, comfortable, and at home with wealth and power, we belong to the world rather than to Christ."

His analysis should be compared with that of Lloyd Billingsley (Reading 2).

Jim Wallis is a founder and pastor of the Sojourners community in Washington, D.C., and editor of *Sojourners*. He has written *Agenda for Biblical People* and edited *Peacemakers: Christian Voices from the New Abolitionist Movement*.

The divisions in the world today are less along the lines of ideology than they are along the lines of power. Our times have seen a growing conflict generated by the disparity between the rich and poor of the world, between those who

Jim Wallis, *Agenda for Biblical People* (Harper & Row Publishers, Inc., 1976). Reprinted by permission of the author.

have power and those who do not. The central questions in the arenas of struggles for social justice concern the need for redistribution of wealth and power on a global scale.

The world's most powerful nations share a desire for economic and military domination that surfaces in startling structural and political similarities between the huge capitalist and socialist bureaucracies.

When the Soviet Union rolled its tanks into the streets of Prague and crushed the stirrings of independence in Czechoslovakia, the Soviets claimed an inherent right to prevent a country from slipping out of their orbit. That same doctrine operates at the heart of American foreign policy, as has been so brutally demonstrated in Vietnam and elsewhere in the Third World. When an insurgent social movement or a new government threatens to take a nation out of the United States' economic, political, and military orbit, the American government's often-claimed commitment to self-determination for other countries quickly shows itself to be without substance. When American policymakers believe that business, diplomatic, or strategic interests are threatened by a development in another country, the United States assumes the right to conspire unilaterally and act against that threat through economic reprisal, political subversion, assassination, paramilitary, or military operations. The same tactics are used in aggressively subverting "unfavorable" regimes and in creating circumstances in which American economic and political power is protected and promoted. Both American and Soviet powers have acted to create and maintain client regimes in other countries that exercise control through means of repression, terror, and torture. A totalitarian spirit fuels the engines of both Wall Street and the Kremlin.

The Influence of Corporations

American policy is dominated by the vested interests of an increasingly concentrated corporate power structure that seeks greater control throughout the world with a coherent global strategy to help create and stabilize a system of "open societies" in which United States economic, political, and military interests can operate more or less freely. This Pax Americana is reminiscent of another "peace" from another time. Arnold Toynbee, the British historian, comments:

> America is today the leader of a world-wide anti-revolutionary movement in defense of vested interests. She now stands for what Rome stood for. Rome consistently supported the rich against the poor in all foreign communities that fell under her sway; and since the poor, so far, have always and everywhere been far more numerous than the rich, Rome's policy made for inequality, for injustice, and for the least happiness of the greatest number. America's decision to adopt Rome's role has been deliberate, if I have gauged it right.[1]

The causes of revolutionary war and violence are not primarily conspiracies and outside agitation, but are rooted in the economic and political institutions of the United States and other major powers and in the values and attitudes of the people of the rich nations. Throughout its history, the United States has been characterized by a continuous expansionist thrust, first in striving for territorial acquisition and, more recently, in seeking economic and political control and domination. That same expansionist pattern has dominated the history of the other powerful nations of the modern world.

The expansionist thrust has always been represented as a noble effort to advance "freedom," "democracy," "civilization," or some other great value. The obvious questions that come to mind are: Freedom for whom and freedom for what? Who are the chief beneficiaries and who are the victims of these advances in "democracy" and "civilization"?

Cloaked in their own self-righteous rhetoric, the powerful nations in history have actually been engaged in self-interested empire building. A foreign policy designed to expand American profit and power in the world has never been affected by the changing of presidents and is a working assumption of both political parties. Concluding that "national security" comes only in dominating others, American leaders have created a society organized for war since 1945.

We have watched the United States conduct military and paramilitary campaigns around the world. Less visible ways of intervention include the support of dictatorial regimes that protect American interests; the training of local military and police elites in the effective "control" of social revolution; and the use of terror, torture, assassination, and economic and political subversion.

The United States' enormous and far-flung commercial interests and worldwide deployment of military power have brought the growth of elaborate networks and systems of espionage and secret political offensives, of expanded research and development in methods of warfare and counter-insurgency, of huge public relations and propaganda campaigns designed for mass persuasion, of the militarization of science, and of the mobilization of the universities, all adding to the arsenal built to protect an empire.

Wealth and Power

The key concept is control. The rich nations have sought to create, on a global scale, those conditions and relationships that guarantee the protection and expansion of their economic and political power. By aggressive investment and trade, by maneuvering the weaker nations into dependent relationships, by use of financial arrangements, military agreements, and political alliances with local elites, the rich nations have forged an empire. It is an empire based upon the influence and control of the political economies of the nonindustrial nations rather than upon territorial conquest and is, therefore, "invisible," an empire without boundaries.

"We are the number one nation," said President Lyndon Johnson at a crucial point in the Vietnam War, "and we are going to stay the number one nation." He was merely articulating an honest and accurate definition of the doctrine of national interest as interpreted by American leaders and policymakers. Staying number one is a struggle for permanent victory that requires the United States to pursue its national interest at all costs.

The United States, being the richest and most powerful nation, becomes, as Martin Luther King charged, "the greatest purveyor of violence in the world." This happens by virtue of the necessity of protecting American wealth and power in the midst of the world's poor and exploited masses. A dependence upon violence in its many forms is inherent in being "number one," and the public's willingness to acquiesce when the call is sounded to support "the national interest" is crucial. The uncritical acceptance of the myth of "the national interest" and "national security" is essential in keeping the United States the number one nation.

The system of empire is based upon the consumer society. The constant pressure for an expanding Gross National Product (GNP) and rising standard of living justifies and requires commercial expansion and the use of political and military power to secure expanded openings for American businessmen around the world. Our ever-growing consumer society is thus at odds with world peace. An international economic system that keeps huge sectors of humanity at a subhuman level while permitting the minority to consume most of the world's resources can only result in conflict. Peace is possible only if the poor and weaker nations of the world are willing to accept the present distribution of wealth and power and the rules of the game as laid down by the United States and the other powerful nations. The alliance of multinational corporations and the military and political strength of the world's most powerful governments have forged the empire that upholds the consumer society.

We are finally coming to understand a discomforting but central fact of reality: the people of the nonindustrialized world are poor *because* we are rich; the poverty of the masses is maintained and perpetuated by our systems and institutions and by the way we live our lives. In other words, the oppressive conditions of life in the poor countries, like the causes of poverty and misery in our own land, are neither merely accidental nor because of the failures of the poor. Our throw-away culture of affluence and wasteful consumption fragments and privatizes our lives. Our consumer orientation lulls us into primary concern for ourselves, and into a passive acceptance of the suffering of others.

Hunger and disease due to hunger are today responsible for two-thirds of the deaths in the world each year. It is estimated that a child born in the United States today will consume, during a lifetime, twenty times as much as a child born in India, and will contribute fifty times as much pollution to the environment. Of every one hundred babies born in the world, forty will die before age six. Another forty are at risk of permanent physical and mental damage because of malnutrition. Only three out of that hundred will get the education and skills they need to perform creative and meaningful work. While those in the rich nations worry about the potential for violence in the rebellion of the poor against the status quo, they fail to recognize the violence inherent in established structures and relationships that inflict injustice and agony by relegating the poor to subhuman conditions of life.

We have learned much about the United States through the eyes of the disadvantaged, the black, brown, red, and poor white minorities locked in urban ghettos of human misery, in rat-infested tenements, and in rural prisons of poverty. Race and sex are still the basis for denying people their basic human rights, and class and color continue to be the primary factors in determining a person's share of justice, education, health, respect, income, and society's goods and services.

All this is aggravated and intensified by the growing concentration of economic and political power in the hands of a few persons and institutions. Certain people, classes, and institutions possess an enormous and illegitimate amount of power that is exercised for their own benefit. This power is, at root, economic, and comes to dominate and corrupt the political process. In the United States, such power is centered in the small number of large corporations that shape the political economy. The decision-making of these large corporations is in the hands of the very few and the very rich.

"Free Market": An Illusion

To suppose that corporate decisions are subject to the forces of the "free market" or to a meaningful sense of public accountability is to engage in illusion. These multinational corporations have gained great power and are increasingly able to act unilaterally in national and international affairs. American society itself is organized according to the large corporate model, and corporate interests and profits dominate production, distribution, communication, information, education, technology, entertainment, and, of course, politics.

We confront a socio-economic-political system based on the dominance of the few over the many. The affluent lifestyle of the American people supports such a system at home and around the world. John Woolman, an early American Quaker, once said, "May we look upon our treasures, the furniture of our houses, and our garments, and try [*sic*] whether the seeds of war have nourishment in these our possessions."

Yet the Bible contains a mandate to protect the poor from the abuses of wealth and power. The prophets spoke of God's anger with the politics of oppressive affluence:

O my people, your leaders mislead you,
    and confuse the course of your paths.
The Lord has taken His place to contend,
    He stands to judge his people.
The Lord enters into judgment
    with the elders and princes of His people:
"It is you who have devoured the vineyard,
    the spoil of the poor is in your houses.
What do you mean by crushing my people,
    by grinding the face of the poor?" says the Lord God of
hosts.
(Isa. 3:12–15).

The gospel is biased in favor of the poor and oppressed. It presents a call to the church—that body that is most dynamic when it is most a minority living in radical contradiction to the values of the world by its proclamation and demonstration of a whole new order called the kingdom of God. But our churches have yet to grasp that vision. Their lifestyle, social prestige, and relationships identify them with the elite power groups of our society, rather than with the poor and oppressed. Our Christian institutions are often dependent on parts of the American establishment that oppress the poor. To come to terms with the gospel will cost the churches a great deal.

The churches are faced with whether they will continue to align themselves with a world order that subordinates justice and peace to the interests of the American establishment. This choice must be made with the knowledge that such a world order is threatened by the counterviolence of those who are its victims. The consequence of a choice to align with the world order will be endless war, revolution, death, and destruction. Such an outcome is inevitable unless some of those who have benefited from the American world order withdraw their allegiance from it, resist its designs and demands, repudiate its basic assumptions and values, and begin to construct alternatives that will provide a new kind of leadership and direction in the wealthy nations. This mission is one of peace, reconciliation, evangelism, and prophetic ministry—a mission for the church.

God and the Poor

Issues of wealth, poverty, and economic justice are central in the Bible. The sheer bulk of the biblical teaching about the rich and the poor is overwhelming. The Old Testament is filled with it. Jesus talks more about it than almost any other single issue. The apostles regard the relationship to money and the poor as a primary test of obedience to God. The people of God, in both the Old and New Testaments, are seen as offering an *economic alternative* to the prevailing assumptions of the world that surrounds them.

Contrary to the dominant attitude of our own society, one's economic life and standard of living is not a private matter. It is a critical issue of faith and discipleship. Not only is the Bible's teaching on the rich and the poor striking in its quantity, it is uncomfortably plain and clear in its meaning. The Scriptures are not neutral on questions of economics. The God of the Bible is clearly and emphatically on the side of the poor and the exploited.

Throughout Scripture we find an insistence that a vital relationship to God will evidence itself in an active serving of social and political justice as witness to God's gift of life. The prophets warned that piety, proper religion, and ritual observance are inadequate. They demanded economic and political justice. Isaiah tells us that the fast in which God delights involves breaking the yoke of oppression, sharing our bread with the hungry, and bringing the homeless poor into our homes (Isaiah 58:5–7). Amos claims that worship and praise are not acceptable to God unless justice rolls down like waters and righteousness like an ever-flowing stream (Amos 5:21–24).

The coming of Jesus brings social revolution. The down-trodden were objects of Christ's compassion. When questioned if He was the "one to come" from God, Jesus offered proof of his messiahship by His ministry to the concrete needs of the suffering and afflicted (Matt. 11:5). Jesus also warns those who would call His name that they will be judged by how they respond to the hungry, the poor, the naked, the imprisoned, the sick, and the stranger. The parable of the Good Samaritan demonstrates that our responsibility for our neighbor extends to anyone in need, and leaps over the human barriers of race and class at personal cost of time, money, and danger. The apostles repeatedly claim that faith without works that demonstrate obedience is dead, and that the quality of our love for God is shown in our practical and sacrificial love for our brothers and sisters.

Nowhere in Scripture are the rights of the rich proclaimed; nowhere is God seen as the savior and defender of the rich and their wealth; nowhere are the poor exhorted to serve the needs of the rich and be poor for the sake of the wealthy. Throughout Scripture, however, the rights of the poor are proclaimed; God is revealed as their savior, deliverer, and avenger; and the rich are instructed to serve the poor and relinquish their wealth and power for the sake of the poor. Nowhere in Scripture is wealth praised or admired or the rich upheld and exalted over the poor. In many places in the Bible, however, the poor are blessed and uplifted, and the message of God's Word carries with it the hope of justice and liberation for the poor. Riches are seen in the Bible as, at best, a great spiritual danger and, most often, as a sign of sinful disobedience to God. Just because the rich are rich, it will be harder for them to enter into the kingdom than for a camel to pass through the eye of a needle. The gospel is preached to the poor, and the rich are told to see what they have and give to the poor for the sake of the kingdom.

The Bible and Riches

The Bible makes clear that money and possessions are deeply spiritual concerns at the core of human experience and, perhaps, reveal more about an individual than any other aspect of a person's life. The danger of riches in the Old Testament is in the misuse of wealth and power in the oppression and exploitation of the poor. The earth and its fullness belong to God and are given for the life and development of all God's children. The Jewish tradition of Jubilee Year provided for a periodic redistribution of land and wealth that militated against the accumulation of riches. In the thunderings of the prophets, God was powerfully revealed as the God of the poor and dispossessed, pouring out His wrath upon the rich and powerful whose affluence crushed the poor and powerless.

In the New Testament, the teaching on wealth is intensified, and its possession is seen as a great spiritual danger. The possession of wealth twists and distorts people's priorities and values and is a crucial obstacle in their sensitivity to God. The New Testament condemns, not just improper attitudes toward wealth, but also the mere possession of undistributed wealth.

One of the very first tests of discipleship to Jesus Christ is a radical change in one's relationship to money and the possession of wealth. The demands of mammon are completely irreconcilable with a total commitment to God. Jesus says, "You cannot serve God and mammon." Notice that He does not suggest that you should not; He simply says that you cannot. He assumes that the will of God and the demands of mammon directly contradict each other, and loyalty must be given to one or to the other.

If Jesus was so concerned about the danger of money and possessions in a simple agrarian society, how much more do we, living in the most affluent nation the world has ever known, need to break radically with the power and authority of money and possessions in our lives. An affluent church witnesses to its radical dependence upon wealth, not upon God, and has almost nothing to say to the dispossessed majority of the globe.

We need to hear again the words of the New Testament applied with their full force to us. (cf. Luke 6:24–25; Matt. 19:24; Luke 14:33; Matt. 6:19–21; Matt. 6:24; Matt. 25:44, 45; Mark 4:7, 18–19; Luke 12:15; 2 Cor. 8:13–14; Eph. 5:5, 6; 1 Tim. 6:8–10; James 2:14–17).

The "just comfortable" standard of living in the rich nations is a sharp contrast to the lives of the poor of the earth. We must begin to face the harsh reality that everything the Bible says about the rich applies to us. Our overconsumption is theft from the poor. No longer must our words put us on the side of the oppressed and our style of life put us on the side of the oppressors.

God did not give the Americans half the world's resources so that we could be good stewards of it; rather, the Americans have stolen those goods from the poor. Unless we are willing to stand with the oppressed by first breaking our attachment to wealth and comfort, all our talk of justice will be sheer hypocrisy. The stating of principles and good intentions, the denunciations of crying injustices, the endless declarations will lack any weight or moral authority apart from a deep awareness of our responsibility before God and our hungry neighbors.

It is well to remember that the mark of sacrificial giving in the New Testament is not in how much is given but, rather, in how much is left over after the giving is finished

(Luke 21:1–4). We cannot give sacrificially and still remain wealthy. It is critical that we constantly heed the biblical warning against minimizing the cost of a visible, outward break with the power of money and possessions. An affluent church cannot say, "Gold and silver have I none," and neither can it say, "In the name of Jesus of Nazareth, walk!"

The Church: Called to Sacrifice

The church is the body of Christ. This dramatic biblical metaphor speaks of the powerful way the work of Christ has united us to Him and to each other. It means that Christ is alive and present in the community and is head over the body. It means that the church is called to embody the presence of Christ in the world by obeying His words, reflecting His mind, and continuing His mission in the world by following the manner and style of His life, death, and resurrection. Jesus tells us that He came into the world not to be served, but to serve, and so it is with us. Our vocation is to serve men and women in His name. We are called, not to be conquerors, but to be a self-giving body whose leader was crucified on a cross and asks His followers to take up that same cross. We are called, not to accumulate wealth and influence, or to strive to manipulate power, but to empty ourselves as He did for the sake of others.

We are called to give a cup of cold water in His name, which will mean feeding the hungry, meeting the needs of the homeless and refugees, supporting the imprisoned, befriending the lonely, standing with the poor and the outcasts, and loving the unloved. This means confronting with our lives the institutional and root causes of the condition of the oppressed. The life that Christ gives is meant to be spread about, not hoarded for the private edification of believers. The compassion of Christ always resulted in action, and so must ours. John, the apostle, exhorts us:

> By this we know love, that He laid down his life for us; and we ought to lay down our lives for the brethren. But if any one has the world's goods and sees his brother in need, yet closes his heart against him, how does God's love abide in

him? Little children, let us not love in word or speech but in deed and in truth.

By this we shall know that we are of the truth, and reassure our hearts before Him (1 John 3:16–19).

The cross of Christ is both the symbol of our atonement and the pattern for our discipleship. Today, many who name the name of Christ have removed themselves from human hurt and suffering to places of relative comfort and safety. Many have sought to protect themselves and their families from the poor masses for whom Christ showed primary concern. In affluent societies, our approach to social problems is to decrease their visibility. The migration patterns of Christians and their churches have again reflected the dominant social practice. The church's compassionless inactivity stems from being out of touch with the suffering of the poor and exploited. This modern isolation from human hurt is a major obstacle to being faithful to biblical mandates. How can we open our hearts and lives to those whom we have hardly ever seen, let alone ever known?

The biblical idea of love carries with it the deliberate extension of ourselves to others. The incarnation, the supreme act of God's love, required the Lord of Glory to plunge into the chaotic, violent, and rebellious human situation at tremendous cost (Philippians 2:6–11). But this act brought the salvation of the world. We cannot profess the name of Jesus without seeking to incarnate His pattern of self-emptying love and servanthood. This is not only an individual effort, but a corporate one undertaken by a body of people who have given themselves to Christ and His kingdom, to each other, and to serving in the midst of the broken world for which He died.

God entered the human situation as one of the poor and powerless. Thomas Merton, in his *Raids on the Unspeakable*, speaks of the meaning of the incarnation:

> Into this world, this demented inn, in which there is absolutely no room for Him at all, Christ has come uninvited. But because He cannot be at home in it, because He is out of place in it, His place is with those others for whom there is no room. His place is with those who do not belong, who are rejected

by power because they are regarded as weak, those who are discredited, who are denied the status of persons, who are tortured, bombed, and exterminated. With those for whom there is no room, Christ is present in the world. He is mysteriously present in those for whom there seems to be nothing but the world at its worst.... It is in these that He hides Himself, for whom there is no room.

The gospel knows nothing of what sociologists call "upward mobility." In fact, the gospel of Jesus Christ calls us to the reverse, to a downward pilgrimage. Former attachments and securities in the false values of wealth and power are left behind as we are empowered by the Holy Spirit to seek first the kingdom. From an obscure birth in a dirty animal stable, to the crucifixion of a poor suffering servant who never had a place to lay his head, the gospel witnesses to God's identification with the poor and powerless. Such a life of identification will bring rejection from the world, and if one becomes too prominent, one might even be crucified. We may measure our obedience to the gospel by the degree of tension and conflict with the world that is present in our lives. If our lives are secure, comfortable, and at home home with wealth and power, we belong to the world rather than to Christ.

"All Things in Common"

Our downward pilgrimage will drive us to community and is meant to take place in the context of a common shared life. The life of the early Christian fellowships, as seen in the Book of Acts and elsewhere in Scripture, presents the Christian life as a common life, the life of a people more than the life of individuals. Here were the ones who had known Jesus, walked with him, talked with him, listened to him, and lived with him for three years. They had seen him live, die, and rise from the dead. They were eyewitnesses to the gospel. They had both followed him and forsaken him. Their lives had been decisively and irrevocably changed by him. He had set their feet upon a new path, and they would never be the same. In response to his command, they gathered in an upper room to wait for the promised coming of the Spirit.

At the day of Pentecost, they were all in one place, waiting, when suddenly there came a sound like "a strong driving wind," and "they were all filled with the Holy Spirit." The consequence of the outpouring of the Spirit was a bold and mighty proclamation of the gospel, repentance on the part of many who saw and heard, and the establishment of a *common life* among the believers. (See Acts:2:42–47).

The coming of the Spirit *did* result in a common life among the early believers. (See Acts 4:32–35). The holding of "all things in common" was not merely a futile experiment, nor did this practice end at Jerusalem. Rather, common life and sharing are shown throughout the New Testament and became the distinguishing mark of the early church. This shared common life contradicts the ordinary social value that the possession of money and property carries the inalienable right to use and dispose of those assets for one's own benefit. The doctrine of private property as the right to use all of one's material and other resources for one's own purposes is a ruling social axiom; however, this most basic economic assumption is decidedly not Christian. Rather, the descriptions of the Christian fellowships in Acts and elsewhere point to a common use and consumption of resources, assets, and gifts of the body. The key here is the common use according to need, rather than a particular form or legal status of common ownership.

The Spirit had shattered the normal assumptions of the economic order, and the early believers realized that the way of Christ militated against the private use and disposition of resources, and led to the sharing of all resources as needs arose in the community. Material resources, no less than spiritual gifts, were to be shared and freely given for the good of the body, and not for the personal gain and advantage of the one who possessed them. A whole new system of distribution had been created in God's new community, with each person in a process of giving and receiving according to ability and need.

The self-giving of the church, as the history of the early church testifies, happens within the body and also spreads out to any and all who are poor and in need. The people of

God will always and everywhere follow the will of their God and the example of their Lord in serving the poor of the earth. In its life as a servant people, the church is guided by the Holy Spirit and energized by the love of Christ. Jesus Christ is the leader of the new community. In John 17, He prays for the new community:

> But now I am coming to thee; and these things I speak in the world, that they may have my joy fulfilled in themselves. I have given them thy word; and the world has hated them because they are not of the world, even as I am not of the world. I do not pray that thou shouldst take them out of the world, but that thou shouldst keep them from the evil one. They are not of the world, even as I am not of the world. Sanctify them in the truth; thy word is truth. As thou did send me into the world, so I have sent them into the world. And for their sake, I consecrate myself, that they may also be consecrated in truth. I do not pray for these only, but also for those who are to believe in me through their word, that they may all be one; even as thou, Father, art in me, and I in thee, that they also may be in us, so that the world may believe that thou hast sent me (John 17:13–21).

Note

1. "America and the World Revolution," quoted in David Horowitz, *Free World Colossus*, 15.

Reading 2: Radical Evangelicals and the Politics of Compassion

K. L. Billingsley

Radical evangelicals are both ideologically imbalanced and politically irresponsible in their approach to social issues, charges Lloyd Billingsley. The imbalance arises from a refusal to face the whole truth about the causes of poverty and oppression in America and the world. The irresponsibility derives from talk about "compassion" without an understanding of the world as it is. The radical evangelicals' prophetic "compassion for the poor," is, according to Billingsley, notable for its selectivity.

Truth, not propaganda, is the prerequisite for responsible social witness, Billingsley asserts. Evangelicals who would be genuinely compassionate must first be unafraid to face the hard truths about totalitarian regimes.

Billingsley's views should be compared with those of Jim Wallis (Reading 1).

Lloyd Billingsley is a novelist and the author of three nonfiction books, including *The Absence of Tyranny: Recovering Freedom in Our Time* (Multnomah, 1986).

The poor, say those on the evangelical left, are the only ones who have the right to inscribe on their belt buckles, like German soldiers in 1914, the words *Gott mit uns.* Or, as these radical evangelicals usually phrase it: God is on the side of the poor.

People are poor for various reasons, not for one only, but one would never guess this from reading radical Christian publications. For instance, people can be poor because of their own lack of discipline and initiative. A steady provider can develop an alcohol or cocaine habit and plunge himself and his family into poverty. This group gets no sym-

K. L. Billingsley, *The Generation that Knew Not Josef* (Multnomah Press, 1985). Reprinted by permission of the author.

pathy from the Bible at all. In fact, they earn God's judgment.

Other poor people are genuine victims who suffer from injury, disease, or catastrophes such as famine and earthquake. The people of God are commanded to help them, because God is moved with compassion for them.

Still others are poor because of economic exploitation. Slavery is a historical example of this; South African apartheid and the East Indian caste system are contemporary versions. The victims of such exploitation have rightful claim to biblical justice, too.

A final group are the voluntary poor, who willingly give up affluent careers to better serve God and their fellow human beings. With ministerial salaries what they are, pastors could almost be included in this group en masse. Missionaries are another obvious example.[1]

The radical evangelicals, however, view poverty as almost exclusively the result of economic victimization. Somehow, they insist, Western structural mechanisms like an open market and universal suffrage discriminate against the poor; a controlled economy and one-party state such as that of Cuba is deemed by them as somehow liberating and beneficial. Radical evangelicals assume that the free enterprise model is the exploiter. Large corporations also receive the radicals' wrath in spite of the fact that, as Louis Fischer pointed out, Marxist governments are like one huge corporation that controls *everything* and from which there is no escape, as there is from Nestle or Exxon. As Djilas shows, the capitalism that Marxists gripe about no longer exists, but the radical evangelicals do not appear to have noticed. They are living in the past, nostalgic for the days of the dark satanic mills described by Charles Dickens and Karl Marx.

The exploitation model also begs the question of why living standards are higher in free economies than in state-controlled economies. People *flee* closed societies like mainland China for better conditions in free enterprise countries. When refugees leave poor countries such as Mexico or El Salvador, they most often go to the United States, not to socialist Nicaragua. Why is this, if capitalist, open-market, politically free countries are examples of exploitive struc-tures? If socialist dictatorships are so desirable, why must they wall in their subjects? It bears repeating that even Hitler did not need such draconian measures.

Politics as Cure-all

The radical evangelicals' economic exploitation explana-tion for poverty demands a political solution. It assumes that those groups that have risen out of poverty have done so by political means. There is little if any evidence for this, how-ever, as Thomas Sowell shows in *The Economics and Politics of Race.* The overseas Chinese, the Italians in Brazil, the Irish and blacks in America, and the Jews in many countries have generally kept their distance from politics. They have bet-tered themselves economically, Sowell demonstrates, by hard work, thrift, and sacrifice. These disciplines can yield results only in an open economic system. If there is a political solu-tion to poverty, it lies in the option for people to initiate their own economic activity.

The radical evangelicals explain poverty in the lesser developed countries by echoing the Leninist explanation first advanced to show why—contrary to what Marx predicted—capitalist workers got wealthier instead of poorer. Lenin said, in effect, that capitalist bosses were exploiting poor countries and forestalling revolution at home by buying off their work-ers with high wages. Today, this explanation is called the "North-South Economic Dialogue." It fails, however, to ex-plain two things: why the lesser developed countries were poor in the first place, and why those countries that have had the most contact with allegedly imperialistic powers have higher standards of living. The theory is popular only be-cause it advances an explanation of poverty based not on any inadequacies on the part of the lesser developed countries themselves, but only on moral deficiencies on the part of others. As Sowell writes:

> The enduring and fervent belief in imperialism as the cause
> of Third World poverty is difficult to understand in terms

of empirical evidence. But this belief is much more readily understandable in terms of the high psychic and political cost of believing otherwise. These costs are high not only to some people in the Third World, but also to those in the West whose whole vision of the world depends upon seeing poverty as victimization and themselves as rescuers—both domestically and internationally. Many such people assume a stance of being partisans of the poor. But even to be an effective partisan of the poor, one must first be a partisan of the truth.[2]

There is in the radical evangelicals' critique, too, a clear selectivity in the poor they choose to champion. There are certain poor groups that are in their view worthy of love and support—and then there are others that are not. Jacques Ellul, whom radical Christians readily quote when he agrees with them, points out that groups like the Kurds, the Tibetans, and the monarchist Yemenites do not attract the attention of radical Christian groups. Why is this? Are they not as poor as American blacks or the Philippine underclasses? Why do radical Christians find them uninteresting? Ellul has a theory:

> Alas, the reason is simple. The interesting poor are those whose defense is in reality an attack against Europe, against capitalism, against the U.S.A. The uninteresting poor represent forces that are considered passé. Their struggle concerns only themselves. They are fighting not to destroy a capitalist or colonialist regime, but simply to survive as individuals, as a culture, a people. And that, of course, is not at all interesting, is it? But the choice violent Christians make has nothing to do with love of the poor. They choose to support this or that group or movement because it is socialist, anti-colonialist, anti-imperialist etc.[3]

Every issue of *Sojourners* and *The Other Side* magazines bears out this interesting distinction. They support, for the most part, the aristocratic poor who have advocates in the UN and among film stars, such groups as the PLO and SWAPO. They say nothing about the others. Hence, their call to aid the poor lacks credibility.

Is Poverty a Virtue?

Listening to the evangelical left, though, one wonders whether it is even desirable for any people to lift themselves out of poverty. The mindset of *Sojourners* and *The Other Side* reveals a tension between ameliorating conditions of the poor and exalting poverty as a virtue. Theoretically, once people lift themselves out of poverty, they become part of the materialist mainstream and thus fodder for broadsides to "be more concerned about the poor."

At the same time, the magazines declare that poverty is abominable, and they call God's wrath down on us for allowing it (even though Jesus Christ himself said the poor would always be with us). Radical evangelicals also want us to believe that poverty is the only acceptable lifestyle for Christians. But one cannot have it both ways.

The radical evangelical ethic that extols poverty as a virtue is a new version of the 1930s' intellectuals' deification of the proletariat. Arthur Koestler explained how eggheads like himself would willingly eschew their background and learning and lobotomize themselves just to be like Ivan Ivanov—the proto-typical poor worker. Everyone unproletarian was dismissed as bourgeois. Being proletarian can even become a question of wearing the right clothing. Malcolm Muggeridge has described Orwell as decked out in "proletarian fancy-dress." The call to holy poverty is the same sort of social descent.

Can it really be contended that North American and European Christians are not concerned about the poor? American Christians give billions each year in charitable donations. Groups like the Salvation Army have been on the scene at foreign and domestic disasters before anyone else: They are the ones who run missions for derelict alcoholics—a case of the uninteresting poor if there ever was one—not Greenpeace, the Socialist Workers Party, or the Sierra Club. What of the clinics, the counseling, and the hospitals founded by religious groups? What of the acceptance of refugees from countries as diverse as El Salvador and Vietnam?

Yet the March 1983 issue of *The Other Side* derided groups such as the Salvation Army for being "supportive of the political status quo," even though the Salvation Army also operates in Cuba and Nicaragua. In those countries, should the Salvation Army denounce the revolutionary status quo?

Government programs for the poor in the West have tended to be very generous. For example, in the 1970s and early 1980s the only budgets in the world larger than the American allocation for the Department of Health, Education and Welfare were the entire budget of the United States and the entire budget of the Soviet Union. In any case, it cannot be seriously maintained that Western governments do nothing about the poor. They even take in the poor created by their enemies, as demonstrated by the United States' acceptance of the last flotilla from Cuba, many of whose passengers were elderly and handicapped. Theoretically, the marvelous social services of the Cuban state should draw the poor from the four corners of the world.

When there have been earthquakes and natural catastrophes in various parts of the world, many Western nations have rushed material aid, medicine, and personnel to the scene. When Mount St. Helens devastates a huge portion of a state or when a tornado destroys 90 percent of a Wisconsin town, what Third World country constantly accusing the United States of being a grasping exploiter is there lending a hand? None. Western capitalistic nations, to their great credit, have continued to feed the hand that bites them. Some Third World leaders such as Julius Nyerere, whose country of Tanzania has received more aid than any other, have used transfers of funds to consolidate their own power, persecute their enemies, and continue economic experiments which have miserably failed.

All this is not to suggest that Western societies and their economic systems are perfect; but as the record shows, they tend to outperform their scientific socialist counterparts when it comes to providing for the poor.

None of us, especially those like myself who see a small role for government, should rest on our laurels. We need to be constantly exhorted to do more for the poor, within the church and without. God commands us to do so. Whether the evangelical left holds the moral qualifications to make this exhortation—along with its occasional appeal for donations for its own programs—remains to be seen.

When Jesus saw the multitudes, the Gospels tell us, he was "moved with compassion."[4] The face of the Savior must have had a way of radiating His inner feelings. In another place we are told that Jesus, beholding the rich young ruler, "loved him."[5]

"Compassion" is a beautiful word, but it is now so debased as to be barely usable. Politicians have been largely responsible for this. The late David Lewis of the socialist Canadian New Democratic Party based his 1974 election platform on a call for a "Compassionate Canada," with the adjective in this case meaning, "More control by a government of its citizens' resources." The American Democratic Party describes itself as "the party of compassion." The word in this connection has come to mean something like "the willingness of a representative to spend other people's money." Those unwilling to spend at acceptable levels are charged with "lacking compassion."

The "Boat People": Whose Fault?

Jim Wallis outlined the radical Christian position on compassion in a September 1979 *Sojourners* editorial about Vietnamese refugees entitled "Compassion Not Politics for Refugees." Wallis conceded that the suffering of these people was "real," hardly an original revelation. He understated their perils, though, by neglecting to mention marauding Thai pirates who preyed on the refugees and sank their ships. He went on to say that it is important to "get the facts straight" and that the coverage of the boat people was "filled with inaccuracies, myths, misconceptions, and outright lies," though he neither mentioned nor refuted any of these with facts of his own. The situation, we are told, "is complex and highly politicized and does not lend itself to easy explanations."

The shift away from simple explanations represents a change for the radical evangelicals. During the Vietnam War, it was very simple indeed: If you favored the American-South Vietnamese side, you were wrong; if you favored an American pullout and the victory of the North, you were right. It was simplicity itself. You were either part of the problem or part of the solution. But now easy explanations are eschewed, though Jim Wallis goes on to advance one himself. Did the Vietnamese government, by any chance, have anything to do with this problem? Perhaps a bit. Their policies, wrote Wallis, were "harsh." One should pause a moment here and contemplate this adjective.

When the Reagan administration, a government elected by an overwhelming majority, put forth its 1980 budget, the cover of *Sojourners* thundered, "ASSAULT ON THE POOR." Its writers readily use pejorative terms such as "militant," "oppressive," "reactionary," and "right-wing" for those who disagree with them. But when a revolutionary government strips people who merely want to leave with all their belongings, extorts outlandish "exit fees," then shoves them off to sea in rusty tubs that barely float, all this merits the description "harsh," something one might say of an overbearing high school principal. What word would *Sojourners* use if West Germany sent its Turkish minority packing on rafts in the North Sea? It would probably not be "harsh." But there is more.

After this scolding, Wallis said the Vietnamese government "must take more responsibility for the orderly and safe exit of those who choose to leave." One looks for terms like "right" and "wrong" here, but the government simply must take "more responsibility," whatever that means. "In this respect," Wallis continues, "the revolution has become the regime and has begun to behave like governments everywhere." Really? Do governments everywhere do this kind of thing to potential emigrants? Does Iceland? Sweden? Belgium? Uruguay? As it happens, only socialist, revolutionary governments such as that of Vietnam have made crossing borders a tricky procedure, particularly on the way out.

It is not long before Wallis gets around to those who are, in his view, really responsible for the refugees—the people of the United States, of course, even though the boat people problem happened after the American forces left—something that Wallis urged for years.

Western Values Caricatured

Slipped into all this is an amazing sentence about the refugees themselves that should be read over several times, preferably aloud, and as slowly as possible. It says a great deal about radical evangelicals' compassion:

> Many of today's refugees were inoculated with a taste for a Western lifestyle during the war and are fleeing to support their consumer habit in other lands.

Notice the sweeping generality ("many") applied to those who were inoculated with this criminal taste for Western lifestyle. And what does Western lifestyle mean? A tendency toward democracy? Mickey Mouse T-shirts? Freedom of religion? A large welfare budget? Abundance of the necessities of life? What? The imagery is that of the addict, fleeing to support his habit. The conclusion is inescapable: many of the refugees to some degree *deserve* what they are getting. Their crime was to be "inoculated with Western lifestyle." This, *Sojourners* would have us believe, merits banishment in leaking boats.

Imagine this scenario: You are a Vietnamese refugee, drifting on a derelict freighter in the South China Sea. Water is low, food almost nonexistent. You have no medical supplies or resources of any sort. Speedboats appear, full of heavily armed Thai pirates who rape the younger women, take some prisoner, steal everything they can find, murder some people outright, then sink the ship. You are left treading water, the cries of the drowning ringing in your ears. Wouldn't it be comforting to know that in secure, faraway America, the editor of a radical evangelical magazine, in an editorial about "compassion," is announcing to the world that you are a Western junkie, fleeing to support your consumer habit in other lands?

The November 1979 edition of *National Geographic* reported that Hong Kong officials picked up a pregnant woman and her child who were in two inner tubes being pushed through shark-infested waters by the woman's swimming husband. The consumer addiction of this group was indeed serious. Doubtless they were after that color television set denied them under socialism.

Wallis denounces then-Vice President Walter Mondale for calling the Vietnamese government callous and arrogant and ends his editorial with, "Our response to the refugees must be one of active concern for the refugees, not out of political self-interest, but out of the compassion of Christ." All in all, quite a performance.

Wallis's statement on the boat people is a piece of poltroonery that ranks with the most bigoted and vicious. It is similar to Anna Louise Strong dismissing the murder of kulaks on the grounds that Russia could get along without them and explaining that Uncle Joe Stalin, after all, had only authorized what the people were already doing. The kulaks too, I suppose, in refusing collectivization, had thus inoculated themselves with the Western lifestyle. Then, too, it has the ring of *Pravda* statements about "rootless cosmopolitans" who have the nerve to leave the Soviet Union.

One wonders what, by these standards, constitutes an attack if Wallis's editorial, as claimed, expresses compassion. *Sojourners* does give us some clues. In February 1980, Danny Collum reviewed Bob Dylan's *Slow Train Coming* album. On one of the cuts, "Gonna Change My Way of Thinking," Dylan says he is going to "stop being influenced by fools." This was too much for Collum, who called it "accusatory" and "downright mean." One would almost think that Dylan was in the process of fleeing to support a consumer habit. Has the government of Vietnam ever been "downright mean"? Or just "harsh"?

Other questions arise: What of the Central American refugees pouring into the United States? Are they, too, fleeing to support a consumer habit? Should they stay at home and be happy in poverty? It hardly need be said what the implication is for those of us who live in the West.

Radicals and Compulsion

Compassion? When a radical evangelical alludes to compassion, he really means compulsion. The *Sojourners'* attack on helpless refugees betrays a tunnel vision that is almost clinical. There is an ideological fungus on the political retina of radical evangelicals that blinds them to the faults of the dour Stalinists who currently run Vietnam. Before they would make any negative statements about a revolutionary (good) government, they attack the moral integrity of the victims of that government. It is assumed that the Vietnamese who remain are bound to do what they are told, even forced labor, euphemistically described in other *Sojourners* articles as "participating in the building of a new society." In the meantime, for the radical evangelicals, it is up onto Rocinante and off at a gallop to the next crusade on behalf of the downtrodden and oppressed through whose plight the United States can be denounced.

Michael Novak was once something of a radical Christian. As an antiwar activist, he even wrote speeches for George McGovern. When asked in an interview why he had changed his stance, he answered:

> One thing that encouraged me in the direction, in fact necessitated this direction, was the destructiveness of radical politics in foreign affairs. The terrible plight of the Cambodian people, the boat people of South Vietnam, and the extraordinary suffering of the people of Vietnam today, have led me to realize that those of us who called for the end of the war in Vietnam unwittingly did something terrible. We caused even more destruction and more suffering, and we are guilty of the consequences of our actions. The least we can do is to learn from such things.[6]

Here is a man who, facing the facts, admits that he was *wrong* about Vietnam. No such admission has been forthcoming from the radical evangelicals. This is a bit surprising.

At other junctures in recent history, *Sojourners* has been strong on apologizing. In the wake of the Iranian hostage crisis, Wallis wrote an editorial entitled "We Could Just Ask Them to Forgive Us."[7] even though it was the Iranians, not the Americans, who took the hostages. The piece ends, "If our national pride and arrogance prevail over our reason and compassion, we will indeed reap the whirlwind." To apologize for someone else's wrongdoing, then, is to show compassion, according to Wallis.

Perhaps the boat people deserve an apology for the things *Sojourners* has said about them; but, for now at least, being a radical Christian means never having to say you're sorry.

Not All Change Is Progress

Barely anything that appears in publications of the evangelical left challenges the assumption that change is progress. In their view, the worst possible action anyone can take, particularly a Christian, is to defend the status quo in any way. The changes that are urged are of a structural, institutional variety and will, we are told, lead to social justice.

What this "progressive" view lacks is an historical perspective. A status quo composed of a divine-right monarch, an arrogant aristocracy, an authoritarian church, and an all-powerful police force is one thing; a status quo of a government of freely elected officials, a free press, universal suffrage, an open market economy, generous welfare programs, public education, and a police force that must read one his rights before arrest, is something else. Yet the superstition of radical evangelicals is that to challenge the sort of institutions that exist not only in the United States, but also in Canada, Liechtenstein, Belgium, and Holland is "progressive"; to hold that they are adequate is reactionary.

The test for anything is not whether it is progressive, but whether it is right. A preponderant government that simultaneously dominated and took care of everyone was what feudalism was all about. Free enterprise democracy constitutes an improvement on that model. To identify progress with an ever-increasing government that serves as a kind of omnipresent wet nurse is to endorse a return to a modern form of feudalism. André Gide used the same reasoning to describe the Soviet Union: In the Soviet system, the arrogant landowner is replaced by the arrogant bureaucrat.

Radical evangelicals, like mainline liberals, are slow to recognize that good intentions are not enough, that government programs set up to eliminate poverty sometimes only create dependency, and that their main beneficiaries are often administrating bureaucrats. Yet it is the politician who most *talks* about poverty and social justice who attracts the support of the evangelical left. Curiously, many politicians of this description—Teddy Kennedy and Pierre Trudeau, for instance—are independently wealthy.

But a political candidate who is for free enterprise and business does not merit the support of the evangelical left because his *intention* is to help people make profits, regardless of what other benefits accrue to the community as a result of the increased economic activity.

In free societies, people have certain rights: life, liberty, and property, for instance. It is the role of government to guard these rights. The evangelical left confuses rights and goals. Living independent of the government dole, in adequate circumstances, with enough surplus to help others, is an admirable goal, but no one can legitimately demand it as a right: It is the result of hard work—even, in many cases, of making a profit.

Of course, making a simple case for basic economic realities is less rhetorically appealing than denouncing the powers that be in the name of God. The truth is not always spectacular.

When it gets down to models of the kind of progressive societies radicals would have us emulate, the term "democratic socialism" emerges, and Sweden invariably is named.

Yet Sweden is really a confiscatory, welfare-capitalist state. Democratic socialism as applied to, say, East Germany (a/k/a the German Democratic Republic) really means undemocratic socialism. It is hard to believe that people would voluntarily assent to the continued total control of their lives—especially control that resulted in reduced living standards. Democratic socialism—"socialism with a human face"—remains an illusion.

All governments have limits. No system can avoid the foibles of life. In Sweden, Denmark, and Holland, people smell bad, die young, go insane, have car accidents, contract terminal diseases, love each other, murder each other, and commit suicide much like the citizens of Brazil or Nepal.

There are no utopias. The advocacy of increased government control, far from being progressive, leads, as F.A. Hayek wrote, down the road to serfdom. One wonders, therefore, why radical evangelicals lean so hard on political solutions.

Notes

1. R. C. Sproul, "Biblical Economics: Equity or Equality," *Christianity Today*, March 5, 1982, 94.

2. Thomas Sowell, *The Economics and Politics of Race* (New York: Morrow, 1983), 229.

3. Jacques Ellul, *Violence* (New York: Seabury, 1969), 67.

4. Matthew 14:14.

5. Mark 10:21.

6. "Interview with Michael Novak," *The Wittenburg Door*, November 1982, 24.

7. Jim Wallis, "We Could Just Ask Them to Forgive Us," *Sojourners*, January 1980, 3.

Index

165